To Bill & Mary -
Thank you for
being such wonderful
supporters of history!

[illegible signature]
May, 2016

Edwards Place

A Springfield Treasure

Erika Holst

ISBN: 978-0-578-15804-4

Photographic credits:
Garth's Auctions, p. 121.
Anastasia Lowenthal, pp. 49, 117, 123, 125, 128-132, 134-138, 140-145.
Sangamon Valley Collection of the Lincoln Library, p. 2.

All proceeds from the sale of this book benefit historic Edwards Place.

To donate to the restoration, or to order additional copies, contact:
Springfield Art Association
700 N. Fourth St.
Springfield, IL 62702
(217) 523-2631 • collections@springfieldart.org
www.edwardsplace.org • www.springfieldart.org

Printed in Illinois.

R & R Bindery Services
499 Rachel Road
Girard, IL 62640

Dedication

One hundred and eighty-plus years is a long time for a house to survive and thrive. Edwards Place could not have done so without the generations of people who cared enough to donate their time, energy, resources, and enthusiasm to make sure that the doors to this hospitable old home always stayed open. This book is dedicated to them—past, present, and future.

Table of Contents

Edwards Place

Chapter One

Thomas Houghan

AND THE BUILDING OF EDWARDS PLACE

A VERY LONG TIME AGO - before Springfield became the capital of Illinois, before a young lawyer named Abraham Lincoln rode up and hung out his shingle, before the town was anything more than a dusty village clinging to the edge of the prairie – the foundation was laid for a story-and-a-half brick dwelling house that would one day come to be known as Edwards Place. Little could the masons have imagined, as they methodically laid their bricks during that summer of 1833, that the house they were building would stand for more than 180 years, through births and deaths, and marriages; through economic booms and busts, through civil war and world war, through an industrial revolution and a technological revolution. Today, Edwards Place stands as a living monument to all the years it has endured and all the lives it has touched.

The story of Edwards Place starts just two years after Sangamon County was formed in 1821. The federal government conducted the first county land sales in 1823. That year William Kelly, an early Springfield settler, purchased the 80-acre tract of land on which Edwards Place sits for $1.25 an acre.

At that time Springfield's population numbered not more than thirty families. Peter Cartwright, who visited Springfield that year, dismissed the village as "a few smoky, hastily-built cabins, and one or two little shanties called 'stores.'" Commerce consisted of a general store, three taverns, a post office, a government land office, and a horse mill and distillery. The first courthouse was at the corner of Jefferson and Second Streets, and the center of town was concentrated along Jefferson Street from about First to Fourth Streets.

Nine years later, in June of 1832, Kelly sold his 80 acres to Thomas Houghan for the sum of $2,800. By then the appearance of Springfield had started to change. The 1831 construction of a grand new courthouse on what was previously the fringe of settlement shifted the direction of the town's growth south and slightly east, and the public

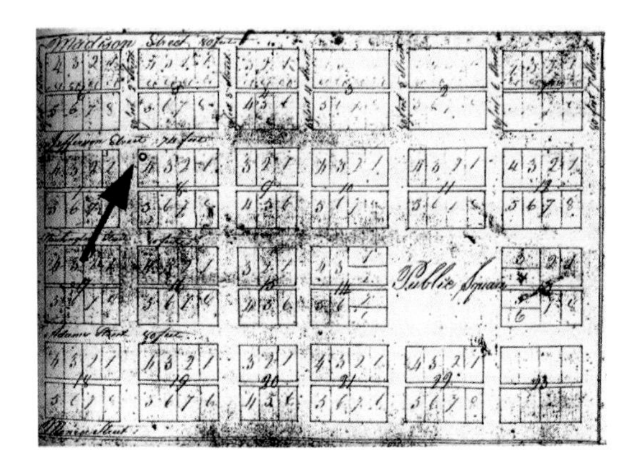

The original plat map of Springfield. The center of town was concentrated along Jefferson Street between First and Fourth Streets.

square eventually became the new center of town. Today we know this square as the location of the Old State Capitol building. The site where Edwards Place would eventually be built was located north of the city limits, close enough to ride into town, yet far enough away that it felt like a country estate.

Houghan had just arrived in Springfield from St. Louis, where he had been a bookseller and stationer in the firm of Essex & Houghan. Houghan's business partner, Thomas Essex, had died of cholera in 1828, and Houghan married the widowed Ann Essex shortly thereafter. He brought Ann and her young son, William, with him to Springfield in 1832.

Born in upstate New York, Houghan was a trained physician, although it is unclear whether or not he actively practiced medicine in Springfield. He did, however, style himself as "Dr. Houghan," and in 1832 he joined seven other Springfield physicians in issuing a public service announcement warning against the spread of cholera.

For the most part, however, Houghan seemed to have made his living through land speculation. Records of Illinois land tract sales show that Houghan entered into 342 land transactions with the federal government, purchasing tens of thousands of acres of Illinois land in 14 different counties. Although the purchase price for this land was only $1.25 per acre (the federal rate for land sales at that time), Houghan had to outlay huge amounts of cash to make these purchases. It is unclear where this money came from. Houghan presumably then sold the land at a profit.

Both Houghan and his wife were active in their religious practice. Houghan was instrumental in bringing the Episcopalian Reverend Charles Dresser to Springfield (years later, Dresser would perform the marriage ceremony between Abraham and Mary Lincoln). On behalf of Springfield's

Episcopalian Church, Houghan wrote a letter asking Dresser to become the new minister and offering him a salary of $400 per year. His wife Ann, for her part, was active in the Springfield Female Bible Society.

In her reminiscences, Helen Edwards indicated that Edwards Place was built in 1833. Archival documents indicate that this date is likely accurate. When William Kelly sold his land to Houghan in 1832, there was no house on the property. In 1834, Houghan sold a portion of the property to Thomas Jones "reserving, however, thirty acres of the last mentioned eighty acre lot including the present residence of said Houghan."

There are no surviving photographs or drawings of the house as it appeared when it was first built; all that is known about it comes from its footprint, which is still discernable underneath the many subsequent additions. In its earliest incarnation, the house consisted of a kitchen, dining room, center hall, and two parlors, with three bedrooms in a half-story upstairs.

Remnants of the house which date to 1833 still survive today, including original oak floors in the dining room and old kitchen; plaster strengthened with horsehair covering sections of hand-riven hickory lath; straight-sawn joists, and walnut trim, doors, and mantels likely constructed from black walnut trees harvested on the property.

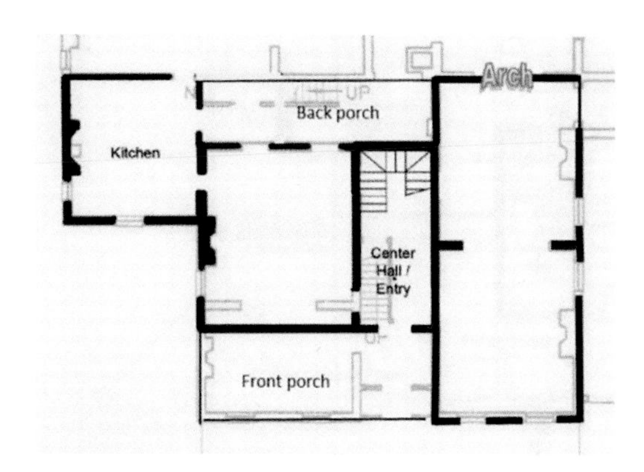

The original footprint of Edwards Place as it was built in 1833.

Original architectural details still survive in Edwards Place. Left to right: straight-sawn oak joists, walnut trim, and hand-riven hickory lath.

Springfield was architecturally unremarkable in the early 1830s. When William Cullen Bryant passed through Springfield in 1832, he wrote that "the houses are not so good [as those in Jacksonville], a considerable proportion of them being log cabins, and the whole town having an air of dirt and discomfort." A year later, another traveler described Springfield as "an irregular village of wooden houses." In contrast to the log and small frame houses that comprised most of Springfield's built environment, the spacious brick Houghan house would have had an air of distinction and stability. As leaders of the fledgling community, the Houghans clearly felt that they needed a distinguished dwelling.

In contrast to the log and small frame houses that comprised most of Springfield's built environment, the spacious brick Houghan house would have had an air of distinction and stability.

Oral tradition about Edwards Place held that the house was originally built with a detached summer kitchen, which we now know as the "children's parlor." It was generally surmised that the summer kitchen was connected to the rest of the house when Edwards Place underwent expansion and remodeling in 1857. But new research has made it clear that the summer kitchen and its adjoining room (now known as the library), were constructed as a single unit that formed an early addition to the original dwelling. Early 19th century details such as hand-riven hickory lath, a sandstone foundation under the children's parlor, and walnut trim in the library suggest that the addition

Next page: Artist's rendition of how Edwards Place may have appeared when it was first built in 1833. *Illustration by William Crook.*

William Crook Jr. 2013

$1000 REWARD!!!

GROVER'S IMPROVED PATENT *COOKING STOVE*, *for Wood or Coal*.—We challenge the State of Illinois, on a forfeiture of One Thousand Dollars, to produce a Cooking Stove, that will compare with the above named Stove, in point of convenience, economy and cheapness.

Should any of our citizens still have doubts of its utility, convenience and economy, we would refer them to Dr. THOMAS HOUGHAN, of this place, who has had one of the above stoves in use for several weeks past.

Springfield, Oct. 1, 1836. H. E. BRIDGE & CO.

Thomas Houghan bought and endorsed a cooking stove in 1836.

The footprint of Edwards Place after the c. 1836 addition of a summer kitchen and dining room.

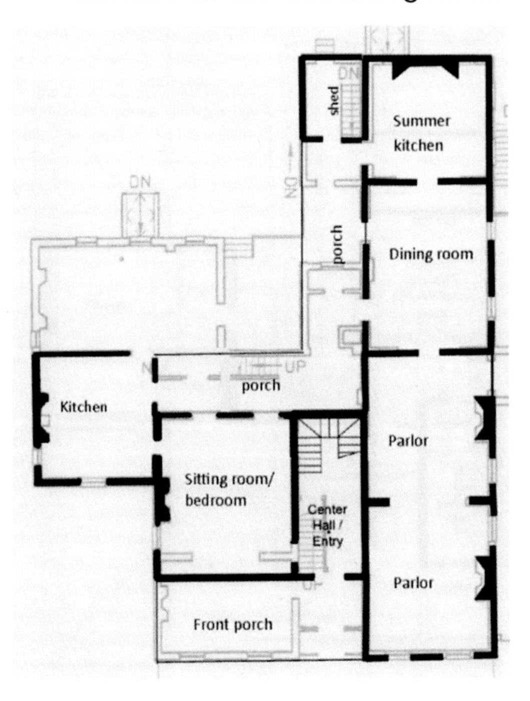

predates the 1843 start of the Edwards family's occupancy.

But when, exactly, was this addition made? The answer to that question is suggested by an advertisement for Grover's Patented Cooking Stove in the *Sangamo Journal* which first ran on October 1, 1836. The ad touted the stove's benefits and mentioned that Thomas Houghan "has had one of the above stoves in use for several weeks past." Because summer is an excellent time to undertake a construction project, and the building of a new kitchen is an excellent time to purchase and install a new cooking stove, this advertisement gives strong evidence that Houghan added the summer kitchen and adjoining room in the summer of 1836. This would also date the addition to one year before the Panic of 1837, when Houghan's credit probably dried up, along with much of the country's. Houghan used the original kitchen during the cold winter months and used the new summer kitchen to keep heat and smells away from the living areas of the house during the hot summer months. The new room adjoining the summer kitchen was likely used as a dining room.

Pieced together from the gathered evidence of disparate sources, a picture emerges of Thomas Houghan as an upstanding but mysterious citizen who was active and respected in the community. Houghan served on the Board of Directors for the State Bank of Illinois and the Board of Commissioners for both the Wabash and Mississippi Railroad and the Sangamon Fire Insurance Company. He was even appointed as a commissioner to superintend the construction of the new statehouse, though he declined to serve and another man was appointed in his place.

Houghan was also a member of the Illinois Agricultural Society, who awarded his horse, Isabella, a prize in 1835 for the "best 2 year old filley." Three years later, in October, 1838, Houghan alleged that some Potawatomi

Indians being marched through Springfield on the Trail of Death had stolen one of his mares, which wound up in Indiana. The stolen horse might well have been the prize-willing Isabella. Houghan spent two years corresponding with people in Indiana unsuccessfully trying to recover the mare.

Politically, Houghan was a Whig. On June 3, 1840, the Whigs organized a huge rally in support of William Henry Harrison, their presidential nominee. A procession two and a half miles long and fifteen thousand people strong marched through downtown Springfield, shouting, waving banners, and playing music. After snaking its way through town, the procession finally arrived at Houghan's grounds for an afternoon of barbeque and speeches.

SPRINGFIELD, Ills., JUNE 5, 1840.

OUT POURING OF THE PEOPLE!!

YOUNG MEN'S CONVENTION,

AND OLD SOLDIERS' MEETING.

A staunch Whig, Houghan hosted a huge pro-Harrison rally at his estate in 1840.

Thomas Houghan sold the house known as Edwards Place in 1843 and moved his family back to St. Louis. The citizens of Springfield heard little of him until 1864, when they were stunned to learn that Houghan's legal wife was

The citizens of Springfield were stunned to learn that Houghan's legal wife was not Ann but Sophia, a woman he had abandoned in his native New York...

not Ann but Sophia, a woman he had abandoned in his native New York, and that Sophia was suing more than 300 residents of Springfield for her dower rights to all Houghan's land transactions.

According to the details of Sophia's lawsuit, Thomas Houghan was born Thomas Hughan in Guilford, New York. Regarded as a "young man of peculiar talent, genius, and learning," he was apprenticed to a local physician, Colby Knapp, and sent to live in Knapp's household. Hughan married one of Knapp's daughters, and the couple went into housekeeping across the street from her father. They had two children; one who died in infancy, and a daughter named Louisa who survived. Being "unused to business," Hughan experienced financial difficulty and was eventually sent to debtors' prison. Upon his release, Hughan fled to South America, leaving his wife and daughter behind in New York. After several years, Hughan turned up in St. Louis under the name "Houghan," where he became a bookseller and eventually married his deceased partner's wife – a marriage that, by virtue of his marriage to Sophia, was not ultimately legal.

Meanwhile, back in New York, Louisa Hughan was taken in and raised by her maternal aunt and uncle, who were childless, while Sophia alternated between living at her father's house and going on extended visits to friends in Connecticut and New York City. Around 1827, Sophia's relatives in New York were alerted to her deteriorating mental condition and she was brought home. Her "derangement" consisted of "choosing to dress oddly" and "roving abroad to make visits to friends at improper seasons." The superintendent of the local asylum pronounced her "incurable." She lived for a time with her sister and

apprised she is quiet and inoffensive,
her aberration consisting in choosing
to dress oddly and rove abroad to
make visits to friends at improper
seasons – in the belief that her family

Houghan's abandoned first wife, Sophia, was deemed a "lunatic" by her friends and family for "choosing to dress oddly."

brother-in-law, Lydia and Daniel S. Dickinson, the same couple that raised her daughter Louisa. Louisa, who had grown into an "exquisitely delicate and beautiful woman", eventually married her uncle's law partner, Ausburn Birdsall, and Sophia went to live with her daughter and son-in-law.

Tragedy befell Thomas Houghan and his family in the 1860s. His "second wife," Ann, died in 1860, as did his daughter, Louisa Hughan Birdsall. Houghan himself died in 1862. And poor "lunatic" Sophia was left in the care of her daughter's husband, Ausburn Birdsall, who found himself resentful of the financial burden Sophia imposed on him.

Acting on Sophia's behalf, Birdsall initiated a series of lawsuits. By this time Birdsall was a very prominent man, as was Sophia's brother-in-law, U.S. Congressman Dickinson, and the suits he filed made the newspapers from New York to California. Birdsall sued Thomas Houghan's estate, administered by his stepson William Essex, for $5,000 as compensation for the 20 years of room and board Birdsall provided to his mother-in-law. The judge awarded Birdsall $850. Birdsall also sued the St. Louis Orphans' Home, which had been a beneficiary of Houghan's estate.

Sophia Hughan's brother-in-law, Hon. Daniel S. Dickinson, gave testimony during her lawsuits describing her marriage to Thomas Houghan and his subsequent abandonment of her.

The most sensational of Birdsall's lawsuits was filed in Illinois to recover Sophia's dower rights. Under 19th century Illinois law, a woman was legally entitled to one-third of her husband's estate when he left no will. During real estate transactions, a woman had to voluntarily relinquish her claim to the land being sold for the transaction to be considered valid. When Thomas Houghan sold land in Illinois, Ann Houghan signed off on the transactions, but because she was not legally his wife, hers was not the required signature. Sophia Hughan, the woman Thomas was still legally married to, had no idea that Thomas was selling land and therefore she never relinquished her dower rights.

In the 20 or more years since Houghan had bought and sold land in Illinois, those parcels of property had been resold and subdivided numerous times. Birdsall's suit named more than 400 people in Springfield as defendants; each one of them possessed a piece of property that Houghan had once owned.

Each defendant was issued a subpoena summoning them to court. Those that responded, showed up, and presented their case were relieved from their obligation to Sophia. Those who did not show up had their property surveyed by the court and were ordered to pay Sophia the cash value of the disputed land.

Were it not for Sophia's lawsuits, the truth about Thomas Houghan's identity would have remained lost to history...

Sophia netted a significant sum of money from these lawsuits, yet New York Census records indicate that, in 1870, she was living in a lunatic asylum. By 1880 she had returned to the household of her former son-in-law, Ausburn Birdsall, who had since remarried. She died shortly thereafter. Were it not for Sophia's lawsuits, the truth about Thomas Houghan's identity would have remained lost to history.

Edwards Place

Chapter Two

The Edwards Family

OF EDWARDS PLACE

WHEN BENJAMIN AND HELEN EDWARDS purchased Edwards Place in 1843, he was a twenty-five-year-old, newly-minted lawyer and she was his twenty-four-year old wife and mother of three-year-old Helen Maria. The couple paid $4,000 for their house. It was an enormous sum for the time; a year later the Lincolns would buy a story-and-a-half frame cottage for $1,500. But Benjamin and Helen were no ordinary young couple. Benjamin was the youngest son of former Governor of Illinois Ninian Edwards, and thus a scion of one of the most prominent families in the state.

PATRIARCH: GOVERNOR NINIAN EDWARDS

Ninian Edwards was born in Maryland in 1775 to Benjamin and Margaret Beall Edwards. His father, though a planter and merchant by trade, was very active in public life: he was a member of the state convention of Maryland that ratified the Federal Constitution, a member of the first United States Congress, and a member of the Maryland General Assembly. Ninian, following his father's example, also pursued a life of public service. Trained as a lawyer, he moved to Kentucky at age 19 to manage some family land. There he quickly became one of the state's leading men, successively serving as a state representative, circuit court judge, presidential elector, and chief justice of the Kentucky Court of Appeals. In 1803, he married Elvira Lane, his twenty-six-year-old first cousin from Maryland.

When the Illinois Territory was organized in 1809, President James Madison named Ninian Edwards its Territorial Governor. Just 34 years old at the time of his appointment, he was the youngest man ever to govern Illinois as either a state or a territory. Like many of Illinois's early governors, Ninian Edwards was a slaveholder. When Ninian and his family moved to Kaskaskia, Illinois, they brought a number of slaves with them.

During his nine years as territorial governor, Ninian made a good deal of money through several profitable

Governor Ninian Edwards, the Edwards family patriarch.

ventures, including farming, land speculation, and investment in sawmills, grist mills, and stores. When Illinois was accepted into the Union in 1818 as the 21st state, Ninian was elected a United States Senator. After his term ended, he was elected Illinois' third Governor in 1826.

Constitutionally limited to one term in office, Ninian Edwards returned to private life in 1830 when his term as Governor was over. After losing a bid for the U.S. House of Representatives in 1832, Ninian devoted himself to charitable medical work in Belleville, giving free care to local residents. He died in an 1833 cholera epidemic at the age of 58.

SIBLINGS: NINIAN W., ALBERT, AND JULIA

Ninian Edwards's legacy included a vast fortune in land and a family of professionally successful, socially prominent children. His oldest son, Ninian Wirt Edwards, studied law at Transylvania University in Kentucky. Ninian W. moved to Springfield in 1835 and spent the majority of his professional life in public service, serving as Illinois Attorney General, a several-term member of the Illinois House of Representatives, and the state's first Superintendent of Public Instruction. His wife, Elizabeth Todd, was Mary Todd Lincoln's sister. The Lincolns met, courted, and married in Ninian W.'s home, which was torn down in 1917 to make way for the office of the Illinois Secretary of State.

Governor Ninian Edwards's second son, Albert Gallatin Edwards, also distinguished himself professionally and socially. He was trained at West Point. During his brief stint in the army he was stationed at Jefferson Barracks, Missouri, where he met and married Louisa Cabanne, a daughter of one of St. Louis's oldest families. Louisa died at age 30 in 1841; nine years later, Albert married Mary Jenckes, with whom he had three children. During the Civil War,

Albert served as a Brigadier General in the Missouri State Militia. Just six days before he died in 1865, Abraham Lincoln named Albert Assistant Secretary of the Treasury. Albert retired from the treasury in 1887 and four months later formed a brokerage firm with his son. That firm, known as A. G. Edwards, was in operation until 2007, when it was sold to Wachovia, Inc.

The Governor's daughter, Julia Catherine Edwards, married a rising star on the national political scene. Daniel Pope Cook had been a newspaper editor and clerk of the Illinois Territorial House of Representatives who used his influence to push for Illinois statehood. In 1818 he was elected to the U.S. House of Representatives, where he served three terms. While in office he helped to procure a grant of government lands to aid in the construction of the Illinois and Michigan Canal. He was also instrumental in defeating a proposed constitutional convention which aimed to legalize slavery in Illinois. Cook County, Illinois, was named in his honor. Frail of health, Cook died in 1827 at age 33. His wife died three years later. The couple left one son, John Pope Cook, who went on to become a Union general in the Civil War.

Ninian Wirt Edwards.

Albert Gallatin Edwards.

BENJAMIN STEPHENSON EDWARDS

Benjamin Stephenson Edwards was the Governor's youngest son. He was born in Kaskaskia on June 3, 1818. Benjamin was educated at Yale University; when he graduated in 1838 he was the first native Illinoisan to do so.

Benjamin's entire professional career was devoted to the law. After completing his studies at Yale, he clerked under Stephen T. Logan, one of the best attorneys in Springfield. He was admitted to the bar in March, 1840 at age 22. His first two law partners, E.D. Baker and Justin Butterfield, were both luminaries in the Springfield legal profession. In 1843, Benjamin formed a

Benjamin Edwards as a student at Yale University, c. 1838.

partnership with John T. Stuart that remained unchanged until 1860, when the firm of Stuart & Edwards took Stuart's new son-in-law, Christopher C. Brown, as a partner. The firm continued to thrive, eventually becoming one of the largest and most lucrative in central Illinois. It is still in operation today under the name of Brown, Hay, and Stephens.

Although a lawyer by trade, Benjamin also dabbled in politics. Like Abraham Lincoln, Benjamin was a Whig until that party's dissolution in the mid-1850s. In 1856 he campaigned vigorously for John C. Fremont for President, making speeches on behalf of the Republican party throughout Illinois and declaring that he would rather "shake hands with the devil" than join forces with the Democratic party. A year later he became a Democrat, having decided that the Republicans were too radical. His switch to the Democratic Party caused some uproar in Springfield. The Republican-leaning *Illinois State Journal* became very critical of his political activity, accusing him of "sleeping in the same bed as his ancient enemies." During the Lincoln-Douglas contest for Senate in 1858, Benjamin placed himself firmly in Douglas's Democratic camp. On July 17, 1858, Benjamin hosted a large political rally for Douglas at Edwards Place, an event attended by thousands of people. Benjamin also supported Douglas in his 1860 bid for the Presidency and publicly declared that he did not believe Lincoln was fit to hold the office.

Benjamin's own political career flourished in the 1860s. In 1861 he was elected to the Illinois Constitutional Convention. In 1868 he was the Democratic candidate in the Springfield district for Congress, a political race which he lost to his own former law student, Shelby Cullom. In 1869, Benjamin was elected judge of the Thirteenth Judicial Circuit. He held that position for only a year, as he discovered that he preferred the predicable hours, lack of travel, and hefty remuneration offered by private law practice.

Benjamin was, by all accounts, a family man. As he expressed to his daughter Helen, "My desire is to do all in my power to make your mother and my dear children happy at home." His care of his daughters continued after they married. After Helen married Moses Condell in 1861, the couple lived for a time with her parents at Edwards Place. By 1863, Benjamin built a grand, Italianate home across the street from his own for Helen and Moses as a wedding present. Several years later he bought them a farm in Bates, Illinois. He showed similar concern for his younger two daughters. Alice and Benjamin Ferguson were invited to live in Edwards Place after their marriage, where they remained for 19 years. When they finally moved out, it was to a new mansion constructed on a portion of Edwards Place's 14-acre estate. By the time Mollie was married, Benjamin's finances were strained, and he lamented that "I have not even been able to furnish a house for Mollie."

Benjamin Edwards as a lawyer at the height of his career, c. 1870.

Benjamin was also interested in ensuring that his children received a proper education. He told his daughter Helen, "I do love you most affectionately and my love for you makes me the more solicitous that you should improve all your opportunities, and become not only a highly educated but a useful and Christian woman." He sent Helen to Monticello Seminary in Godfrey, Illinois for her education, while Alice and Mollie attended Springfield schools. While he possessed a traditional viewpoint in many respects, he did not place much value on the what society believed were the proper "accomplishments" of a young woman, such as piano playing, embroidery, painting, and singing. In fact, he wrote, "I do think a well informed mind, accompanied by a modest and unassuming manner, an 'accomplishment' (if I may use that expression) far surpassing in importance, both for grace and usefulness, most of the modern

Benjamin Edwards as he appeared at the end of his life, c. 1885.

accomplishments of young ladies of the present day."

Benjamin was a strict Presbyterian who insisted on observing family prayers each morning after breakfast. On Sundays he would tie up the children's swings to prevent them from playing on the Sabbath. Such religious observance extended to the rest of the family. Every Sunday his mother-in-law took all the advertising out of the newspaper so there would be no secular material to read on the Lord's day. The family attended the Second Presbyterian Church until 1862, when they moved to the First Presbyterian Church. Helen frequently contributed baked goods and hosted parties in service of the church, and Benjamin, despite a lack of musical aptitude, served for a time on the church's music committee.

Benjamin's health began to fail in 1885; by January, 1886, it was clear he was not long for the world. He slipped into a coma on February 1 and died four days later. His body was placed on view at Edwards Place, followed by funeral services held at the First Presbyterian Church and interment at Oak Ridge Cemetery. Springfield citizens remembered him as a devoted family man, an excellent lawyer, and a devout Christian. "The loss sustained by this city is an irreparable one," said the *Illinois State Journal* when reporting his death.

HELEN KISSAM DODGE EDWARDS

Helen Kissam Dodge Edwards, c. 1870.

While Benjamin Edwards was a student at Yale University, he became acquainted with a young woman named Helen, younger sister of his classmate Richard Dodge. On August 13, 1839, Benjamin and Helen were married, beginning a partnership that would last forty-seven years, until Benjamin's death in 1886. Helen and Benjamin's acquaintance may have started in childhood, as they lived near each other for a time in Kaskaskia, Illinois as small children. However, family legend has it that Benjamin and Helen's marriage was arranged by Helen's strong-willed mother Jane, and the couple were almost strangers to each other when they married.

Helen Kissam Dodge was born in Kaskaskia on November 14, 1819 to Henry Dodge, a veteran of the War of 1812, and Jane Dey Varick, a descendant of prominent New York Knickerbocker families. The Dodge family returned to New York in 1825, where Henry died of a severe cold in 1827. Helen, her mother, and her brothers moved to New Haven in 1834 so her brothers could attend Yale. Helen attended boarding schools in New York but left after nine months due to ill health. Returning to New Haven, she continued her studies at ladies' schools until she married Benjamin.

A few months after their wedding, the young couple moved to Springfield, Illinois, motivated by a desire to establish their home close to Benjamin's brother Ninian. The newlyweds reached Springfield on the snowy evening of January 4, 1840 after a sixteen-day journey. Upon their arrival, Helen was not pleased with what she saw: Springfield had no streetlights and no sidewalks, and its roads were nothing but stretches of mud. Her attitude changed upon arriving at the home of Ninian and Elizabeth Edwards. There she received a warm welcome, not only from her in-laws, but from Elizabeth's sister Mary

Helen Edwards, c. 1880.

Todd, who was visiting Springfield from Kentucky. Helen and Mary quickly became friends. "She did have a violent temper, and she had always been a good deal 'spoiled,'" Helen acknowledged. Still, she said, "I was attracted to her at once. The sunshine in her heart was reflected in her face." The friendship they formed continued until the end of Mary Lincoln's life.

After a two-week stay at Ninian and Elizabeth's home, Benjamin and Helen moved into a small home on the corner of Fourth and Monroe Streets. Their first daughter, Helen Maria, was born on August 25, 1840. A son, Richard, was born in 1842, but he lived only a short time. In 1843, the little family moved to the house now known as Edwards Place, and two more children soon followed: Alice Jane, born August 11, 1844, and Mary Stuart, born November 15, 1848.

Like her husband, Helen was deeply religious. She admonished her daughter that she must "not neglect the reading of your Bible, night and morning, and never omit saying your prayers, not merely saying a few formal words, but with your whole heart, make known your troubles, your wants to Him who will never turn from those who would truly seek Him." Helen kept a sewing basket and a Bible in every room in case she had some spare time to devote to either, saying "It's surprising how many odd five minutes there are in a day."

Despite early struggles with cooking and housekeeping, Helen became a noted cook and hostess. Her skills evolved in response to the demand that came with marrying into one of Illinois's most prominent families, as Benjamin felt it was his social duty to entertain during sessions of the Legislature and Supreme Court. After her death, Helen was remembered as having "dispensed a generous and beautiful hospitality" at the many parties she hosted.

Previous page: Helen Edwards in the formal gardens of Edwards Place, c. 1895.

After Benjamin's death in 1886, Helen devoted herself to the interests of their daughters and grandchildren. Thomas Condell made Edwards Place more or less his permanent home from the time he was 17 years old and thus served as his grandmother's companion, assisted from time to time by his sisters, who lived at Edwards Place during the school year to attend city schools. Alice and Benjamin Ferguson moved out of Edwards Place in 1883, but as their home was next door, they were still a daily part of Helen's life. Mollie Edwards Raymond and her children were also regular visitors to Edwards Place, and Helen regularly took trips to see Mollie in Evanston.

Helen Edwards was remembered as a woman who "exemplified to an unusual degree the sweetness, the kindness, the courtesy, and the consideration of a consistent Christian life."

Although her eyesight started to fail in later years, Helen's mind remained sharp. She died of pneumonia at home on March, 18, 1909. Her funeral was held at Edwards Place, where "a great profusion of beautiful floral designs and blooming plants was massed in the front parlor," according to her obituary. She was remembered as one of "those grand women who founded the social structure of the town," a woman who "exemplified to an unusual degree the sweetness, the kindness, the courtesy, and the consideration of a consistent Christian life."

Left to right: Helen Maria, Alice Jane, and Mary Stuart Edwards.

THE EDWARDS GIRLS: HELEN, ALICE, AND MOLLIE

Benjamin and Helen Edwards raised three daughters at Edwards Place: Helen Maria, born in 1840; Alice, born in 1844; and Mary Stuart (called Mollie), born in 1848. All three girls were married in the formal parlors, and all remained close to their parents, especially their mother, throughout their lives.

Helen was born seven months after her parents' arrival in Springfield and was the only child to have lived in their first house on the corner of 4th and Monroe Streets. She was also the only child to be sent away to school. At age 15 Helen enrolled in the Monticello Female Seminary in Godfrey, Illinois. This was the boarding school of choice for daughters of Springfield's elite; John T. Stuart's daughter Bettie was one of Helen's classmates, and Stephen T. Logan's girls attended years before. Her curriculum at Monticello was considered rigorous for a girl and included subjects such as math, science, and geography.

On September 25, 1861, Helen married local dry goods merchant Moses Condell, the son of an Irish immigrant. Family friend Mercy Conkling, who

Helen Maria as she appeared shortly after her marriage to Moses Condell in 1861.

attended the wedding, said "The bride looked very well, very handsomely dressed, but as usual, had little or nothing to say to any one but Mose!" The couple lived with her parents at Edwards Place for at least two years. During this time they experienced the birth and death of their infant son, Benjamin Edwards Condell. In 1863 they moved into the grand Italianate house across the street which her father had commissioned for her as a belated wedding present. In 1867 Helen and Moses moved to Kansas to start a farm on a large tract of land owned by Moses's father. They took their two-year-old son Eddie with them and left four-year-old Thomas at Edwards Place in the care of his grandparents. During this time Helen Sr. wrote to her daughter every single week. These letters, preserved in the Condell Family Papers at the Abraham Lincoln Presidential Library, give valuable insight into life at Edwards Place.

The Condells returned to Illinois in 1869 and began a new life as farmers on a tract of land in southwest Sangamon County purchased for them by Helen's father. In the mid-1890s they retired and moved back to Springfield, where they quietly lived out the rest of their lives. Moses died after a fall from a ladder in 1914, and Helen died of natural causes in 1925. They had eight children: Benjamin (who died in infancy), Thomas, Benjamin (stillborn), Ninian Edwards ("Eddie," who died at age 19), Helen, Eliza, Alice, and Mary.

Alice Edwards was the first child to be born at Edwards Place. Unlike her sister Helen, Alice was not sent away to school, but instead studied locally, first at Benjamin Suesserott's Springfield Female Seminary, then at Mrs. S. B. Thomson's Select School for Young Ladies. She finished her education in 1862, Mercy Conkling related in a letter to her son that May: "Miss Alice Edwards has left school, her education as she considers it, complete!"

The year before, when she was just 17, Alice had become engaged to a local banking clerk named Benjamin H. Ferguson. The Civil War postponed their plans to marry. Benjamin served as Captain of Company B of the 114th Illinois Regiment until he was mustered out in the spring of 1864 due to ill health. Alice and Benjamin were married on June 16 of that year and made their home at Edwards Place rather than setting up housekeeping on their own. This was not an unusual choice; many young couples of the mid-nineteenth century chose to live with relatives while saving for a house and furnishings. Not all couples, however, chose to live with their families for 19 years, as Alice and Benjamin did with her parents. This was clearly a matter of personal preference rather than financial necessity, as Benjamin's career flourished. He operated a thriving glass and china business and worked his way up through the Springfield Marine Bank, eventually becoming its president.

After her marriage, Alice largely took over the duties as hostess of Edwards Place, frequently throwing parties for her generation of friends. A dinner party for forty in 1868 was typical of the manner in which Alice entertained. Her mother reported "A rather long table was set in the middle of the dining room, in the center of which was a beautiful arrangement of flowers, and up this table were arranged the uncut cakes, baskets, chicken salad, veal bread, ham turkey, pickles, piles of biscuit, rolls, bread & butter &c, and the top of the sideboard was covered with extra provisions." At another party, eleven years later, Alice hosted lunch for twenty friends: "The table looked very elegantly with Alice's beautiful china, iridescent glasses (looking like colored soap bubbles), flowers, etc. and a very beautiful repast was served of quails and French peas, oysters, Saratoga potatoes, different kinds of salads, pies, fruit, coffee, etc."

Captain Benjamin H. Ferguson married Alice Edwards on June 16, 1864.

James H. Raymond married Mary Stuart “Mollie” Edwards on October 13, 1874.

Alice and Benjamin finally built their own home in 1883, right next door to Edwards Place on land given to them by her parents. They never had children. Benjamin died of a heart attack at his desk at the bank in 1903. In 1913, the widowed Alice donated Edwards Place to the Springfield Art Association and remained actively involved as a member and patron until her death in 1921.

Mary Stuart Edwards was named after the wife of her father’s law partner, though everyone called her Mollie. Like Alice, Mollie attended Mr. Seusserott’s and Mrs. Thomson’s schools in Springfield. In 1868 she served as a member of her cousin Charles Edwards’ wedding party. Robert Lincoln (Charles’ cousin on his mother’s side) also attended this wedding. Mollie lived at home with her parents until her marriage to James H. Raymond on October 14, 1874. James was apparently besotted with his bride; Mollie’s mother observed that “he is the most loving fellow, and devoted husband I ever saw. I tell Mollie to enjoy it while it lasts. He says ‘that will be ‘life long.’” The couple moved to Evanston, Illinois, where James practiced law. They had four surviving children: Edward F., Miner, Elizabeth, and Helena, as well as a stillborn infant and a young son named Arthur who lived less than a year. Mollie died in 1928.

Mr. and Mrs. B. S. Edwards
invite you to be present at the marriage of their daughter
Mary to James H. Raymond
Tuesday evening October thirteenth
Ceremony at eight o'clock
Springfield Illinois.
1874.

An invitation to Mollie and James’s 1874 wedding, held at Edwards Place.

Left to right: Tom, Eddie, and Helen Condell.

THE EDWARDSES' GRANDCHILDREN: THE CONDELLS

Benjamin and Helen were active participants in the lives of their grandchildren, who were frequent visitors to Edwards Place. Daughter Helen's oldest son, Thomas, came to live with his grandparents for a year and a half between 1867 and 1869 while his parents farmed in Kansas. Benjamin and Helen doted on the little boy, as did his aunts. "I do not see what we will do with out Tom, and I cannot bear to think of his going away," Alice wrote to her sister as Tom's reunion with his parents drew closer, "Last night after I went to bed & fairly cried, when I thought how few weeks longer he would be with us. I really think he is the sweetest child that ever lived."

As Tom got older, he and his younger brother Eddie (whose full name was Ninian Edwards Condell, after his famous great-grandfather) would frequently take the train in to Springfield to visit their grandparents. Often the boys acted as couriers, ferrying messages and boxes between their parents and grandparents. Tom rejoined the Edwards household in 1880 to attend school in Springfield. His younger sisters Helen and Eliza soon joined him in their grandparents' household so they, too, could attend city schools.

Tom and Eddie had four younger sisters: Helen (named for her mother and grandmother); Eliza (called "Lilie" when she was young); Alice (named for her mother's sister) and Mary (named for her mother's other sister). Helen was fond of her little granddaughters and often sewed or bought clothes for them and made them presents of dolls. "The dolls I have gotten at last, but do not want to send them until they are nicely dressed, and will try to accomplish this next week," ran a typical letter from Helen to her daughter in 1876. "I bought an apron for Helen and Lilie but will bring them out with me, to send them next time," she wrote in 1880.

The Edwards family was devastated when Eddie drowned at age 19 in 1884.

The Edwards and Condell families were devastated in May of 1884 when 19-year-old Eddie drowned while swimming. He had been a student at Jacksonville's Business College when he and a friend went for a swim in Morgan Lake. Eddie felt a cramp and slipped under the water, despite his friend's attempts to save him. Benjamin Edwards took the train to Jacksonville to collect his grandson's remains, as Eddie's mother was too distraught to make the trip. "Judge Edwards, when he arrived, almost broke down at the sight of his grandson's body," the local newspaper reported. Eddie's funeral was held at Edwards Place, and he was buried in Oak Ridge Cemetery.

Of the five surviving Condell children, only two, Alice and Mary, married and had children of their own. Mary Condell married Springfield pharmacist Noble Hudson in 1902, but their family had a sad fate. After only two and a half years of marriage, Noble died of pneumonia on January 8, 1905 at age 34. He left behind an eight-month-old daughter, Alice, and his wife, who was six months pregnant with their second daughter, Elizabeth. In 1913, Alice died of measles just a few days shy of her ninth birthday. Three years later, in 1916, both Mary and Elizabeth developed measles which turned into pneumonia. They died on the dame day.

Alice Condell married Theodore McCoy of Golconda, Illinois in 1897 and had four children: Henry, Helena, Christina, and Benjamin Edwards. Alice's granddaughter, Helen Caterino, lives in Dallas, Texas, and has very generously provided the Springfield Art Association with several books, photographs, and artifacts relating to the Edwards and Condell families.

Neither Thomas, Eliza, nor Helen Condell ever married. The three siblings remained close to each other and to their grandmother throughout their adult lives. Thomas and Eliza lived at Edwards Place and cared for their grandmother during the last years of her life. After her death, Tom and Eliza spent almost four years sorting through and dispensing with sixty-six years of accumulated family belongings in Edwards Place.

All three of the Springfield Condell siblings were active members of the Springfield Art Association, which took charge of Edwards Place in 1913. Thomas Condell shared his vast collection of ethnographic artifacts with the Art Association through lectures and temporary exhibits. Upon his death in 1929, the entire collection was bequeathed to the Art Association. Helen and Eliza Condell were also devoted supporters of the Art Association. They donated family furnishings and artifacts to Edwards Place and were key contributors to the building of the Condell Studio of Art, which is named in their honor. Helen Condell died in 1950, and Eliza Condell died in 1975 at age 102.

MRS. HUDSON AND DAUGHTER DEAD

PNEUMONIA CLAIMS MOTHER AND CHILD WITHIN FEW HOURS

Tragedy struck the Edwards family again in 1916, when Mary Condell Hudson and her daughter Elizabeth died on the same day.

Next page: Thomas Condell bequeathed his collection of antiques and ethnographic artifacts to the Springfield Art Association. They were placed on display in an upstairs bedroom.

HARRY E NEEF

THE EDWARDSES' GRANDCHILDREN: THE RAYMONDS

After her marriage, Mary Edwards Raymond settled in Evanston with her attorney husband. There the couple raised four children and buried two.

Mary's first pregnancy resulted in the birth of a son, Robert, who lived just one day in July of 1875. Helen went to Evanston to be with her daughter as she recovered from the mental and physical trauma of her experience. "Mollie feels her disappointment keenly, and is lonely in anticipation of lying so long in her room, without having the little one by her, for whom she had cherished such hope, and formed so many plans," Helen wrote to her oldest daughter. However, a year later, Mary welcomed Edwards F. "Ned" Raymond. Helen described her young grandson in this way: "He is not pretty – his eyes are too small, and nose too much of a 'pug', but he has a sweet mouth, fine forehead, and is a good natured, jolly baby, really good...but he is a solid lump – a very heavy child..."

Ned was followed at year-and-a-half intervals by Elizabeth (called "Bess"), Helena, and Arthur. Arthur was born with spina bifida, and the duration of his short life was spent in a desperate quest for healing. In the spring of 1881, Mollie left her three older children with her parents in Springfield and took baby Arthur to New York for medical treatment. They were there for three months, during which time he underwent ten surgeries. He died two weeks after he returned home, on May 22, 1881, at eight months old. A few weeks later his anguished mother wrote "I suppose I will grow accustomed to the dropping out of the little life which I find I loved more than I ever dreamed of when I had him, & when I think of his patient sufferings through the whole of his life it seems more than I can bear."

Four years later, Mollie gave birth to her sixth and last child, Miner.

Previous page: Eliza Condell (far right) and her niece Catherine Jones (far left) in 1953 at a tea in Eliza's honor at the Springfield Art Association. Eliza remained an active supporter until her death.

Next page: Helen Edwards on the porch of Edwards Place with granddaughters Bess and Helen Raymond, c. 1895.

One more tragedy lay in store for the Raymond children: when she was nine years old, Bess cut her leg while roller-skating. The wound became infected, and her leg had to be amputated. Helen went to Evanston to be by her granddaughter's side during the operation, which was performed at home. On May 11, 1887, Helen wrote "Poor Bessie's leg is off and buried. She bore the operation, all think, wondrously well but it was a terrible one...with all the coverings on the floor, oil cloth, sheets, towels etc, the blood soaked through to the carpet."

The Raymond children kept in touch with their Edwards grandparents through the exchange of letters and gifts...

In happy times, Raymond children kept in touch with their Edwards grandparents through the exchange of letters and gifts. In 1879, Helen recounted with delight the arrival of a Christmas package from her Raymond grandchildren, who at that time numbered only three: "a package to 'Grandma and Grandpa from the Midgets' was the first and a letter purporting to be from Ned, Bess, and Helen, was read, offering their pictures for our acceptance, I laughed and almost cried. It is the cutest picture of the three babies I ever saw. Bess, not yet two years old, looks as 'independent as you please,' with an I don't care sort of expression, while Ned looks as though he had said, Why must I sit so still? He has quite a distressed look, yet it is a perfect likeness. Little Helen, in the middle, seems obedient and resigned."

The Raymond children would often visit Edwards Place during the summer holidays. By the time they were old enough to make visits, Benjamin

Mollie Edwards' grandson Miner Raymond III lives in Cincinnati, Ohio.

was at the end of his life and tended toward crankiness. In 1880 Helen wrote of fearing that her husband "could not possibly be patient" with his grandchildren, adding that she kept Ned and Bess "away as much as possible from him." Many years later, Bess would recall her only memories of her grandfather:

> I have only two memory-pictures of him, though I must have seen him often. In one of them he is kneeling in front of his chair at family prayers, talking very firmly to God. The other occasion was on a morning in early summer when the train that brought us to Springfield had arrived soon after six o'clock. We children, delighted to be out of the stuffy sleeper and at the beginning of the long vacation at Grandmother's home on North Fifth Street - we never thought of the place as his - were racing madly through the garden. Grandfather, rigidly erect, with his square-cut beard making him look even more Jehovah-like, was taking his regular before-breakfast walk. He met us - and rebuked us for running through a newly-planted flower bed. That was his only greeting.

Helen, however, was always cheerful and patient with her grandchildren; Bess Raymond called her "my best-beloved, most understanding friend."

Ned Raymond was a lifelong bachelor. Bess Raymond married, and later divorced, Fritz Woodward. She had no children. Helen married Alex Carman and had three children: Alex Jr., Mary, and John. Miner Raymond had two children and moved to Cincinnati, Ohio in the 1910s. His son, Miner Raymond III, still lives in Cincinnati. He has provided the Springfield Art Association a wealth of information about his family history.

Edwards Place

Chapter Three

Edwards Place

IN ITS HEYDAY

BENJAMIN AND HELEN EDWARDS'S PURCHASE OF EDWARDS PLACE in the summer of 1843 ushered in a golden era for the grand home. For almost seventy years, it was the center of the Edwards family's life: the place where children were born, illnesses endured, milestones celebrated, and loved ones died. Thanks to the family's prominence, Edwards Place was also a center of social life in mid-19th century Springfield, hosting politicians as well as luminaries of the bench and bar at frequent dinners and parties. The house was alive with the energy and activity of the Edwards family and their guests; that life echoes through the ages and inspires all who are involved in its restoration to the grandeur and vitality of its heyday.

When the family took up residence at Edwards Place in 1843, "it was lonely indeed," recalled Helen, who said "there was not a house in sight except a little log school house between what are now Enos Avenue and Union Street." The estate was located north of the city limits and was considered "out in the country."

The house they purchased was spacious for its time. It boasted two parlors, a dining room, a kitchen, and a summer kitchen, as well as a room that may have functioned either as a bedroom or a sitting room downstairs, and three bedrooms upstairs. There was plenty of space to house the growing family as well as to entertain.

Helen's early days at Edwards Place were dominated by housekeeping duties, which proved difficult for her. Growing up, Helen had lived in boarding houses with her widowed mother and had no opportunity to learn to keep house. Nothing in her upbringing prepared her for taking care of a home, cooking, or caring for children. Exacerbating Helen's predicament, early Springfield lacked trained servants to help with household duties. "It was almost impossible to get servants," Helen recalled. "I had brought a woman from St. Louis but found her so intemperate that in less than a year I was obliged to discharge her."

This left management of the new home entirely to Helen. A local farmer and his wife did most of the outdoor work on the estate, but Helen was expected to "prepare bacon, hams, sausage, lard, candles, and soap for the long winters, as well as to carry on all the daily work of the household" in keeping with Benjamin's high standards, according to her granddaughter. A story survives of Helen standing "in agony over the churn and the butter that apparently never would come, the tears streaming down her face and into the cream - crying the more because he was sure her husband would notice the extra salty flavor and make stern comment on it!"

Helen had long periods home alone with her children, alternated with periods when her house overflowed with guests...

Benjamin, meanwhile, was busy with his law practice. Just as Abraham Lincoln did, Benjamin traveled the Eighth Judicial Circuit, taking cases throughout Central Illinois. This gave Helen long periods at home alone with her children, alternated with periods when her house overflowed with guests as she was obliged to return the hospitality offered to her husband while he was away. The Edwards family also frequently hosted visiting family members. Benjamin's brother Albert and Helen's brothers Richard and John would come with their families for weeks at a time. Helen's mother Jane also lived with them off and on from the time of Helen's marriage until Jane's death in 1876. At one point daughter Helen wrote "We still have a house full of company, and not much prospect of their leaving...Eleven beds are occupied every night.

Allie is obliged to sleep on a feather bed, thrown on the floor."

Helen's housekeeping situation improved in the 1850s, when she was able to hire Irish and German immigrants as domestic help. A large wave of these immigrants began to arrive in central Illinois starting in the late 1840s, pushed from their homelands by famine and political unrest, and pulled by the lure of cheap land and employment on the railroads and canals and in domestic service. The Edwards family typically employed at least two live-in servants (generally a cook and a maid), as well as a hired man to take care of the carriages and grounds. Helen seemed to have an ambivalent relationship with her hired help. She referred to them as her "family," yet considered them "spoiled" and fantasized that she would "make a clean sweep, of my present family, close the house, and begin anew." Yet she could also be sympathetic to the servants' plight; at one point she gently admonished her daughter to be kind to her hired girl, noting that "girls as well as housekeepers get tired and worn out, and need to be spurred and encouraged." The turnover rate for Helen's servants was generally very high; either because Helen fired them or because they quit and moved on. Ellen Bonner, however, worked at Edwards Place as a cook for more than thirty years, from the 1870s until well into the 20th century. Mrs. Bonner's husband and all three of her children had died in the 1860s, and she no doubt considered the Edwardses as her surrogate family.

At some point around the late 1840s, the Edwards family made a small but important shift in the way they utilized their interior space. When they purchased the house in 1843, it featured a kitchen to the northwest and a summer kitchen to the north. Two key pieces of evidence suggest that, by 1850, the Edwards family abandoned use of the kitchen to the northwest and moved their food preparation activities exclusively to the summer kitchen. First, a

Helen Edwards gave this clock to Ellen Bonner, who served as a cook in Edwards Place for more than 30 years.

cache of archaeological artifacts recovered from the backyard indicates an episode in the 1840s when a large number of kitchen goods were discarded, some of them intact. Such a cleaning episode might well have taken place if the family ceased using one of their kitchens. Second, scraps of French wallpaper with an exuberant Rococo print were discovered in this room under the frame of a closet added to this room in 1857. This placement tells us that the wallpaper predates the 1857 construction of the family's new kitchen. As it would have been highly impractical to put expensive wallpaper into the sootiest room in the house, the presence of this paper suggests that the old kitchen's function evolved from a working space to a living space at some point before 1857. That wallpaper was reproduced and installed in the parlors of Edwards Place during the 2014 interior restoration project.

A collection of 1840s artifacts recovered from an Edwards Place privy, including this jug, ewer, and two jars, suggest that the Edwards family abandoned one of their kitchens before 1850. *Courtesy of the Illinois State Museum.*

As the three Edwards daughters grew older, they were able to help their mother in the household. In a letter to daughter Helen, Benjamin wrote of his expectation that she "take a great deal of the care and responsibility not only of the housekeeping, but of your younger sisters off her mind." Helen went to local schools before being sent to the Monticello Female Seminary in Godfrey, Illinois from 1855-1858. Her parents believed that the value of the education she received trumped the loss of having her at home: "I love to have you with us, but...I feel willing to deny to us the pleasure of having you at home, for your own good," Benjamin wrote to her in 1856. Younger daughters Alice and Mollie remained in Springfield, studying first at Benjamin C. Suesserott's Springfield Female Seminary and then at Mrs. Thompson's Select School for Young Ladies.

Helen Maria Edwards was educated at the Monticello Female Seminary *(below, left)* while her sisters Alice and Mollie went to the Springfield Female Seminary and the Select School for Young Ladies *(below, right).*

SELECT SCHOOL FOR YOUNG LADIES.

Mrs. S. B. Thompson will open a school for Young Ladies on Monday, September 24, 1860, on south-west corner of Spring and Monroe streets.

There will be a *Primary* Department connected with the school.

She would refer to Rev. L. P. Clover, N. H. Ridgely, Esq., Hon. S. A. Treat, J. S. Bradford, Esq., Jas. L. Lamb, Esq.

Circulars giving particulars can be had at Messrs. Johnson & Bradford's Book Store. sep20d1w

SPRINGFIELD FEMALE SEMINARY.

The Fall Term of this Institution will commence on MONDAY, THE 10TH OF SEPTEMBER NEXT.

The course of instruction is as full and as thorough as that of our best Female Seminaries, embracing all that is necessary and desirable for the thorough, practical and accomplished education of a young lady. Especial care will be bestowed upon the instruction in the elementary branches. Scholars of all ages received.

RATES OF TUITION:

Primary Classes ....$5 00 per quarter.
Junior Classes....................................... 7 50 " "
Senior Classes. ....10 00 " "

Complimentary branches: German, $5 00 per quarter; French, Spanish and Italian, each $6 00; Drawing and Painting, $5 00; Music, $10 00.

Semi-annual reports of scholarship, conduct, &c., will be sent to parents Tuition payable quarterly in advance. *No reduction excepting in cases of protracted illness.*

For further information apply to

REV. BENJ. C. SUESSEROTT, Principal.

March 27, 1860.—w1y

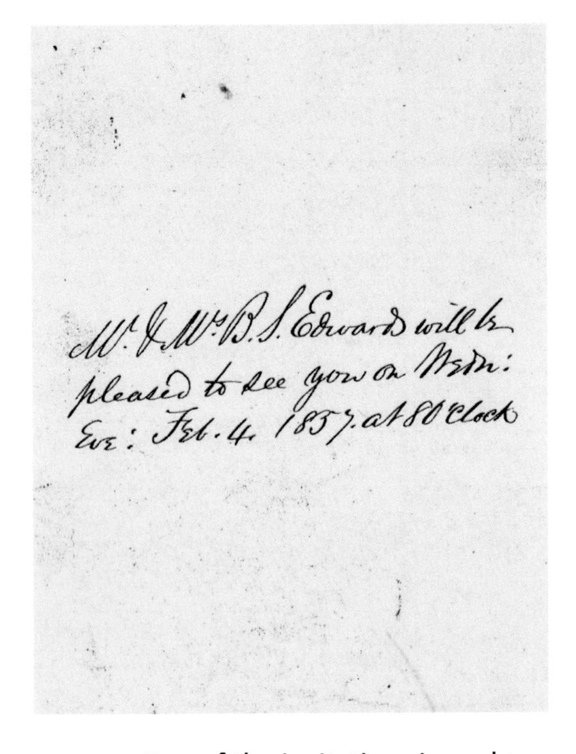

Mr & Mrs B. S. Edwards will be
pleased to see you on Wedn:
Eve: Feb. 4. 1857. at 8 O'Clock

One of the invitations issued to a legislative party thrown at Edwards Place on February 4, 1857.

Edwards Place was also the site of numerous parties. Helen recalled, "Mr. Edwards was very hospitable and entertained a great deal during sessions of the legislature and when the session of the Supreme Court were here." These parties would draw Springfield's society people, all decked out in their finest clothes. The gown worn by Adeline Judd at one of the Edwardses' parties was especially stunning; long after the party, guests could still recall "a corn-colored silk of such magnificence that the soft, lustrous folds of that gown still cast their pale yellow gleam across the length of half a century."

It was the custom of these legislative parties to begin at 8 pm. An invitation to one such party still survives. Written in Benjamin's hand, it said "Mr & Mrs B S Edwards will be pleased to see you on Wedn Eve: Feb. 4. At 8 o'clock". Invitations were issued to all the leading professional and political men of Springfield and their wives. Guests at Edwards Place over the years have included Abraham Lincoln, Stephen A. Douglas, Stephen T. Logan, John T. Stuart, Lyman Trumbull, William Bissell, Richard Yates, Sidney Breese, John M. Palmer, and Ulysses S. Grant, to name but a few luminaries.

The centerpiece of any Edwards party was an elaborate supper. Typical fare included scalloped and raw oysters, salad, bread and butter, biscuits, rolls, pickles, chicken salad, boiled ham, roast turkey, and cakes, which would be spread on a long table. The centerpiece of any fashionable party in Springfield was always confectioner William Watson's famous pyramid of macaroons, built tall and covered with a web of spun sugar. A band would provide music for the guests, though dancing was not allowed due to Benjamin's religious scruples. This did not bother the guests, however; one later recalled that parties without dancing were called "promenade parties," at which "you gossiped and ate and flirted, instead of dancing and eating and flirting."

Many contemporary accounts survive of the Edwards family's parties in the mid-nineteenth century. Giving a glimpse of how active Springfield's social scene was when the legislature was in session, Mary Stuart wrote on January 28, 1855, "last week a party every evening, and sometimes two or three." She continued: "I attended but one, at Stevenson Edwards, it was very pleasant, the two parlors and her large bedroom thrown open for company the table was very handsome, and abundant. Mrs E told me she intended giving a party to the members of their church this week, and wished father and myself to attend." The mention of the "large bedroom" thrown open for company is especially intriguing; it suggests either the dining room or library (as they are known today) was a bedroom before the house was remodeled in 1857.

"I attended but one [party], at Stevenson Edwards, it was very pleasant, the two parlors and her large bedroom thrown open for company the table was very handsome and abundant…" Mary Stuart, January 28, 1855

A few years later, in 1863, twenty-one-year-old Anna Ridgely attended a different legislative party at Edwards Place. She recorded the event in her diary: "I enjoyed the evening quite well. The entertainment was delightful. The supper room was open all evening and the guests walked around the table admiring the delicacies. A band of music enlivened the scene. We did not come home until quite late."

Above: The "Southern Mansion" design from Samuel Sloan's *The Model Architect.* *Below:* Edwards Place today.

Besides hosting legislative parties, Edwards Place was also the site of picnics, teas, and dinner parties. In the summer of 1860, Anna Ridgely wrote that she "went to a kind of picnic at Mrs. B. S. Edwards. It was very warm and we did not go until after ten. It was delightful out there. The girls were all walking in the grove. It looked so nice and cool. The house is new and furnished elegantly."

Anna's comment about the house being "new" is undoubtedly a reference to the significant remodel of the house that the Edwards family undertook in 1857. By then in his late 30s, Benjamin Edwards was a highly successful attorney and a man of influence. He desired a home that reflected his prominent social and professional standing. That summer, he commissioned the prominent Chicago architectural firm of Boyington and Wheelock to create plans for a remodeled home. The architects' drawings envisioned an Italianate villa double the size of the existing structure, with a three-story tower in front and large, circular staircase in the center of the house. The Edwards family must have found the cost of this house prohibitive, because these plans were never realized. Instead, the Edwards family hired the Springfield contracting firm Sutton & Bro. to remodel the house according to the "Southern Mansion" design in Samuel Sloan's *The Model Architect,* an architectural pattern book published in 1852.

Work began in the summer of 1857. Miraculously, several of the contractor's receipts for the work on Edwards Place survived. These documents sat, forgotten, for nearly century in a barn on South Second Street until William R. Stoppelwerth bought the property in the 1940s and discovered them. Recognizing that they might have historical value, Stoppelworth held on

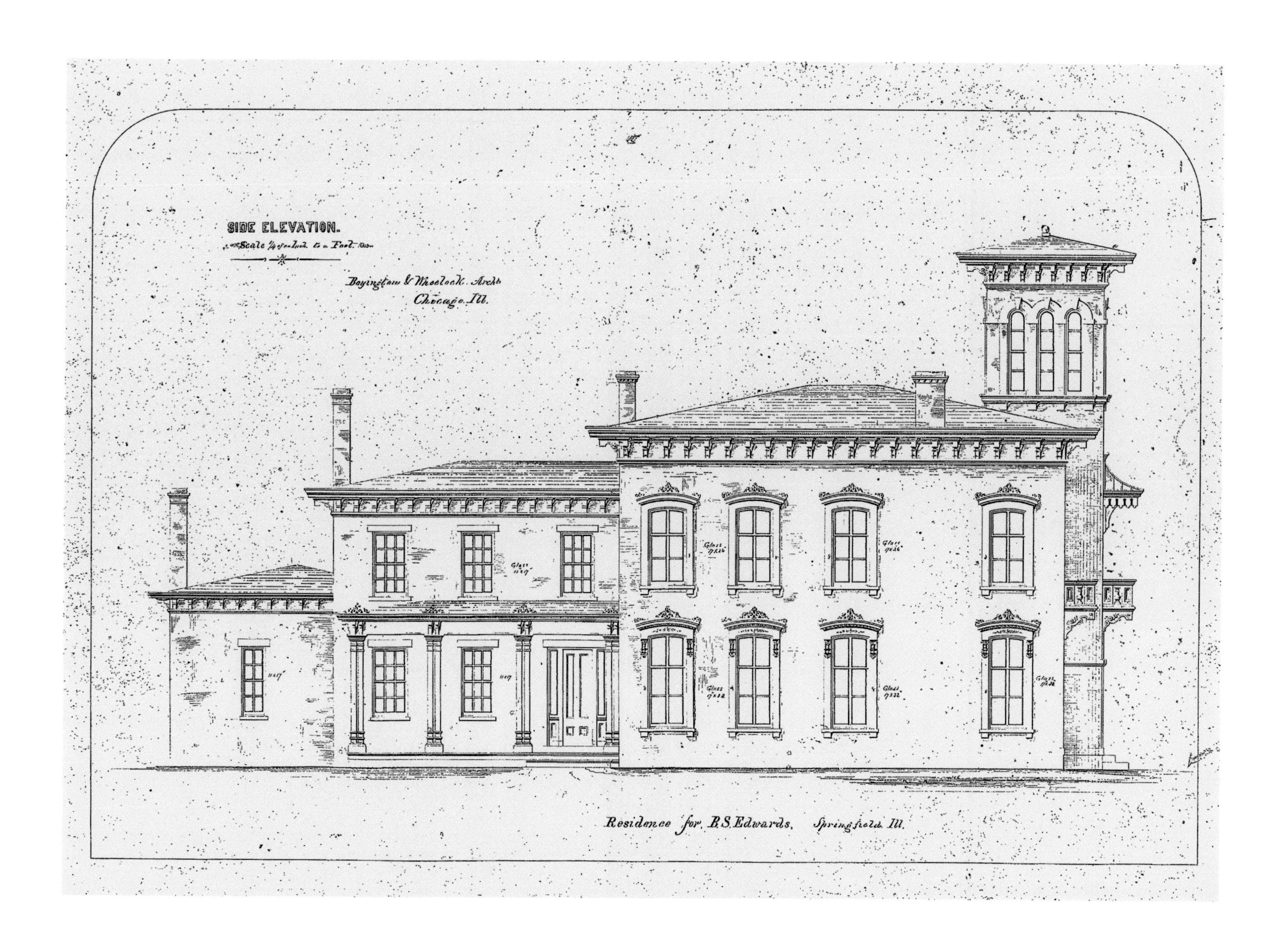
SIDE ELEVATION.
Scale ¼ of an Inch to a Foot.
Boyington & Wheelock Archts
Chicago. Ill.
Residence for B.S. Edwards, Springfield. Ill.

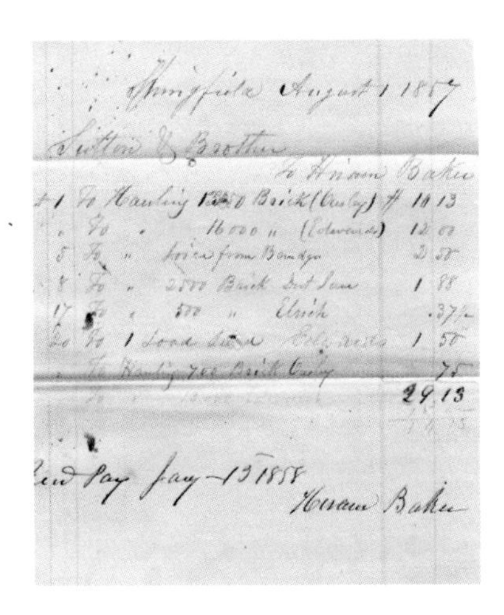
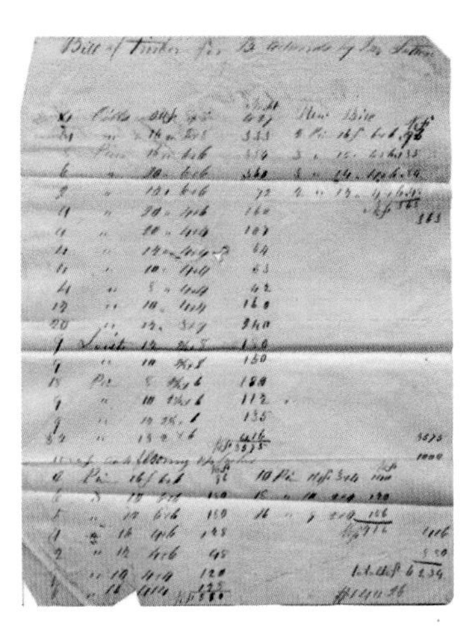
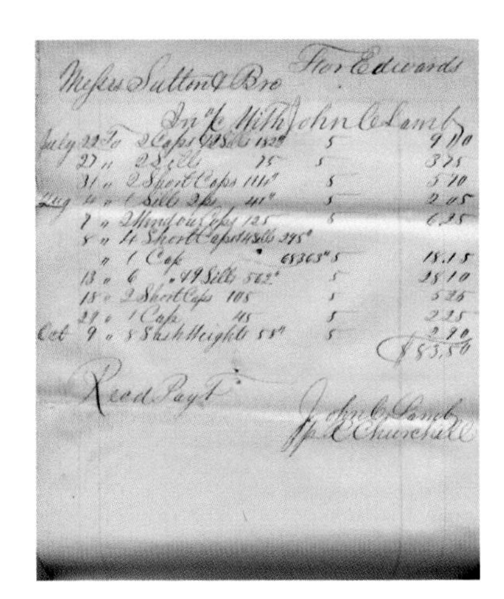
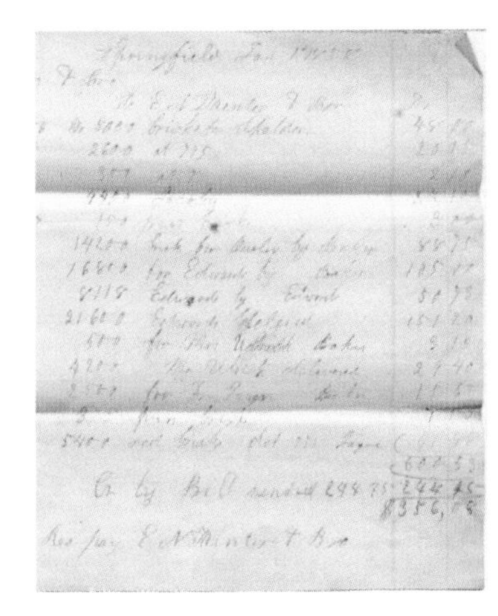

A cache of documents pertaining to the 1857 remodel of Edwards Place came to light in 2012.

to the documents. After Stoppelwerth's death in 2009, the documents passed to his children, Sheryl and William ("BJ"), who sold them to the Springfield Art Association in the winter of 2013. The documents include bills for timber, fitting windows, hauling bricks, and digging out a new cellar. They provide such valuable bits of information as the fact that 1,000 feet of ash flooring was installed to the fact that 44,000 bricks were used to the exact date the new kitchen range was installed in 1857.

When the work was completed in the fall of 1857, Edwards Place was transformed from a story-and-a-half, vernacular Greek Revival dwelling to a two-story Italianate mansion. The Italianate style appealed to the Victorians' love of he picturesque and sentimental by evoking the architecture of Italian Renaissance villas. Popularized through pattern books published by the architect Alexander Jackson Downing, this style first made its appearance in the homes of Springfield's elite in the 1850s, and continued its popularity through the 1870s. Classic characteristics of the Italianate style which can be seen on Edwards Place include low, hipped roofs; bracketed eaves; a cupola; tall, narrow windows; a balustraded balcony; and an emphasis on verticality.

Although the 1857 remodel dramatically changed the house's outside appearance, inside, the footprint changed very little. Notable changes included

Previous page: Grandiose plans to remodel Edwards Place were drawn by Boyington & Wheelock of Chicago in 1857 but never realized.

the creation of a new sitting room in the southwest corner of the first floor, the transformation of the back porch into an enclosed servants' hall and staircase, and the construction of a full second-story and spacious attic. The kitchen at the north end of the house was also replaced by a new kitchen and laundry wing to the northwest. The fireplace was removed in the old kitchen and a chimney for a parlor stove added, and the room became a playroom for the children.

The remodeled house included some important technical innovations. Benjamin Edwards was a charter member of the Springfield Gas Works, and he made sure that his house was fitted with pipes to provide gas light in each of the rooms. Gas light provided illumination equivalent to 15 candlepower; a six-arm chandelier burning as brightly as 90 candles at the twist of a valve must have seemed like a miracle. Five original gas chandeliers still hang in Edwards Place today. The new kitchen boasted a state-of-the-art cooking range, while the basement laundry featured sinks and a boiler to heat water.

With regard to finishes, the Edwards family incorporated some new trends while retaining much of the home's original character. As the first place a visitor would see and form an impression within the house, the front hallway logically received the most stylish trim, in this case Italianate-style pine which was faux-grained to resemble oak. The Greek Revival walnut mantel in the dining room was replaced by a Rococo-style cast-iron mantel patented just a year before, in 1856. The Greek Revival walnut mantels in the parlors were replaced by elegant white marble mantels, and a white marble mantel was installed into the front sitting room. The Edwards family chose to retain the original Greek Revival-style walnut trim in the parlors and library. The former summer kitchen, which became a children's parlor, was fitted with pine trim that was faux-painted to match the original walnut trim. These additions and

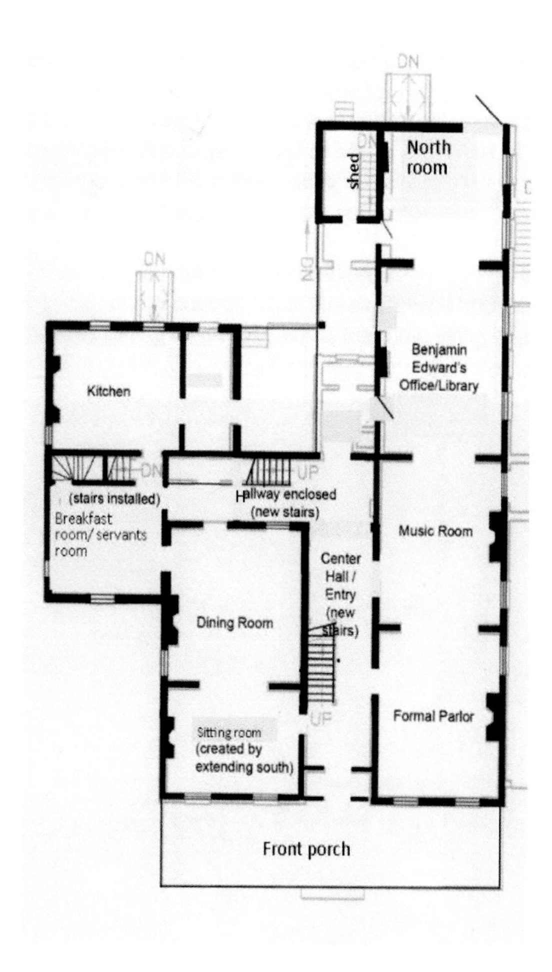

The footprint of Edwards Place after the 1857 remodel. Although its appearance changed dramatically, very little new space was actually added.

Stylish details added in 1857 brought Edwards Place a new standard of refinement.

renovations at Edwards Place brought a new standard of refinement, placing the home among the largest and most luxurious in the city. They enabled the family to host their bevy of socially and politically prominent friends in high style. Within the elegant parlors, social, political, and professional networks were formed and strengthened.

Three of the happiest social occasions to take place in the house were the weddings of each of the Edwards daughters. Helen Edwards married Moses Condell on September 25, 1861. Mercy Conkling, who was present at the wedding, wrote her son about the event: "I have attended Hellen Edwards wedding, a week from last Wednesday, and a terrible night it was. Very dark and rainy, yet notwithstanding, I went with no one but Anderson, and so dark that you could not see the horses head, but do not imagine I was the only one so venturesome. No indeed! The rooms were quite pleasantly filled. And though so gloomy without, all seemed to participate in the joy of the occasion, and the evening passed very delightfully."

Three years later, Alice Edwards married Benjamin Ferguson. The pair had been engaged since 1861 but had postponed marrying when Benjamin enlisted in the Union Army. Benjamin mustered out of the army due to ill health in April of 1864 and married Alice on June 16. Anna Ridgely wrote in her diary: "Thursday night we again went to a wedding. Alice Edwards and Ben Ferguson were united together in a bond to be broken only by death. The affair was a splendid one. Everything was elegant. The house was thrown open and filled with guests. The bride was lovely in her beautiful attire and white silk, lace, and pearls." Another attendee wrote that the wedding was "grandest affair of the kind that ever took place in the city."

"Alice Edwards and Ben Ferguson were united together in a bond to be broken only by death. The affair was a splendid one. Everything was elegant. The house was thrown open and filled with guests..."

Anna Ridgely, June 16, 1864

It was ten more years before youngest daughter Mollie's turn came to be a bride. By the time she married, Mollie was nearly twenty-six, which made her close to spinsterhood. In the end, she chose young attorney James H. Raymond (called "Harry") of Evanston as her husband. The *Illinois State Register* called this wedding "one of the events of the season in fashionable circles in this city," and commented that "Mr. Raymond is surely fortunate in securing so lovely and so excellent a wife."

In between the joyous celebrations of Alice's and Mollie's marriages, Edwards Place hosted a house full of company on the tragic event of Lincoln's funeral. Helen recounted that "our house, being on the road to the cemetery, was thrown open, our rooms were all occupied, cots being put in the library and back room even, to accommodate friends who came from Kentucky and elsewhere, and on the day of the funeral we kept a collation spread the whole day for any who wished to come for refreshment."

Lincoln's assassination came as the grim coda to a long and terrible war. Although far removed from the battlefields, the Edwards family felt the effects of war personally. For a time they had only to look out their front door to be reminded that their nation was in conflict. In 1861 the house across the street was turned into a cartridge factory, churning out 15,000 rounds each day. Behind the factory, a company of soldiers made their camp. Helen felt that

Abraham Lincoln's funeral procession passed by Edwards Place on the way to Oak Ridge Cemetery on May 4, 1865.

these soldiers were "a protection during these troublesome times." But no encampment of soldiers could ease their minds about their loved ones in harm's way: Alice's soldier fiancé was on the front lines, most notably at the six-week-long Siege of Vicksburg. Several of Benjamin Edwards's relatives who lived in the South wrote letters reporting the hardship and suffering in their war-torn section of the country. And the family experienced a personal tragedy in the depths of war when Helen and Moses Condell, who were residing at Edwards Place with her parents, lost their nine-month-old son Benjamin. The funeral was held at Edwards Place on Friday, March 13, 1863.

After the conclusion of the Civil War, life settled back into its customary rhythms at Edwards Place, with a few changes. Helen and Moses Condell went to Kansas in 1867, leaving their four-year-old son Thomas at Edwards Place. Benjamin encountered some financial setbacks. In 1868 Helen wrote "'Times are getting very hard,' and Father is beginning to talk strongly of economy, &c, and has shut us down, with regard to making bills any where even at Bunn's store." Benjamin's financial situation had not improved a decade later, when he wrote to tell daughter Helen he would not be able to lend her money: " Nothing gives me more pleasure that to be doing for my children, but I am too hard run even to make support for myself unless I can soon sell some property. I am broke." It is likely that Benjamin was a classic case of being "land rich but cash poor." He owned considerable property, including Edwards Place and his estate, but after the Civil War he seemed to be bringing in a reduced income with few liquid assets to fall back on.

Helen and Moses Condell left their 4-year-old son Thomas at Edwards Place in 1867 while they established a farm in Kansas.

After her marriage in 1864, Alice and her husband moved into Edwards Place, and Alice assumed the role of hostess within the household. *Standing :* Benjamin Ferguson. *Seated:* Alice Edwards Ferguson and Helen Edwards.

In spite of Benjamin's financial situation, the Edwardses remained one of the most socially prominent families in Springfield, and they continued to entertain in high style. After her marriage in 1864, Alice stepped forward and assumed many of the hostess duties within the household. She delighted in throwing parties for her friends. At a supper party in 1869, Helen reported "there were between forty and fifty here – mostly Alice's old friends...with a few pleasant strangers. It was one of the merriest parties I think I ever saw together. The supper proved fine – oysters splendid, ice cream of Fitzgerald's best, and all did ample justice to it." In 1876, Alice and her mother joined forces to host a "Centennial Party" for their church in honor of the hundredth anniversary of the Declaration of Independence. Their gathering included a "1776 table" with "old-fashioned" food such as "roasted pig at the head, baked beans, cold meats, baked potatoes, corn pose (old fashioned) dough nuts, seed cake, pumpkin pies, pickles, cheese, etc. etc. mush and milk" and an "1876 table" with "modern dishes" such as scalloped oysters, chicken salad, as well as a "curiosity shop of revolutionary relics." As Alice grew more comfortable in her role as hostess, the scale and detail of her entertainment expanded. In 1881 Helen reported "Alice is out making calls on some of the strangers and is greatly inclined to give a party for perhaps a hundred and fifty."

One of the biggest social events of the year at Edwards Place was New Year's Day. As one Springfield resident recalled, "New Year's Day was universally a fête day – everybody kept 'open house'... Each lady received in her own home, assisted by her daughters and any house guests." The Edwards family observed this old-fashioned custom each year, rising early to prepare a tempting array of goodies to offer their callers. A letter Helen wrote on January 2, 1880 describes a typical New Year's Day at Edwards Place:

Our table did look elegantly, and I wish you could all have been here to see it. The center piece was Alice's epergne, the top dish containing large brilliant red flowers, with white intermixed and garlands of smilax going from it to the chandeliers above. Alice's elegant china and all sort of nice things on the table, deviled crabs, "snappers," in which were furry caps and hats, scalloped oysters, sandwiches, rolls, biscuits, cold turkey, jellies, cake, an "angels food" cake from Chicago, but I forgot to say the three dishes of the epergne were filled with oranges, grapes, and apples. The ice cream was perfectly delicious, thanks to you. I thought when I saw the quantity of viands on the table, I could send a nice basket to you of some of these. But last night when the banquet was over, there was precious little left, every sandwich gone, every scrap of angels food, every snapper of which we had four dozen, almost all the cake and grapes, every spoonful of ice cream! And Mrs. Bonner says she never had as little from the plates to throw out as yesterday. We had about one hundred and thirty callers, and more than two thirds had a hearty meal, and I thought there would be loads left. We had a black waiter who was stylish. He arranged every thing in most beautiful manner- spoons and forks, all in form, every thing placed just rightly, and he proved the most efficient helper we ever had, though Ellen was top in the dining room, and "Bunn" (the black) referred to her for every thing extra he wanted. He kept

the table after each crowd going out beautifully. The parlors were handsomely decorated with flowers and wreaths from the folding doors, and many compliments were paid to our table and lovely bright rooms. The girls were lovely, as pretty and nice a company as I would want. Eva was very pretty in blue silk and diamonds, Sallie in lovely blue silk, with a great deal of elegant lace, and Kittie Lanphier in black and cloth of gold, was exceedingly pretty. Katie Hay was bright and handsome. She had a short blue silk and her friend a beautiful young girl, white swiss. Alice Bunn and Mary Burlingham were a pretty duo and enjoyed themselves amazingly, I wish little Helen could have been with them. Mrs Irwin whom I dreaded, had a good day and did ample justice and all the good things. Mrs Bonner did most splendidly, and all the girls- Nellie Shannahan, little Maggie did good work. But yet it don't pay! Except for the pleasure it gives to others.

By 1881, sixty-one-year-old Helen seemed to have grown weary of the effort involved in New Year's Day, grumbling in a letter to daughter Helen "I am very sorry, that I have undertaken this thing, of receiving calls on New Years day. It is a great deal of trouble and expense, and the pleasure does not justify the amount of fretting incurred." Nevertheless, "Alice seems to think we ought to be hospitable on that occasion," so Helen yielded and opened her doors to company again. After Alice moved out, she began hosting New Years' open houses at her own house, though Helen came over to assist.

Life in Edwards Place grew quieter in the 1880s. In 1883, Alice and Benjamin Ferguson moved into a home of their own, albeit directly next door to her childhood home. In 1886, Benjamin died after a year-long decline of health. Though Helen, her three servants, and grandson Tom were the only permanent occupants of Edwards Place from then on, Helen's other grandchildren were always coming and going. The Condell children came to live with her for months at a time so they could attend Springfield schools, and the Raymond children came to spend summers with her. Bess Raymond recalled that her grandmother "liked nothing better than to help a dozen young girls dress for a ball. In later years when my sister and I were there, she always sat up in bed reading till we came in. She was genuinely eager to hear all about it - what she wore and what he said, and how so-and-so's affair was coming on." At the end of her life, Helen's eyesight failed, and Tom and Eliza Condell moved in to Edwards Place to care for her. Eliza recalled that her grandmother "would write, but I would have to guide her by placing her fingers on the line."

Helen's death in 1909 marked the end of the Edwards family's residence at Edwards Place. For the next four years the house sat empty, while Tom and Eliza undertook the task of sorting through and disposing of more than sixty years of the family's accumulated belongings. It wasn't until 1913 that Edwards Place was again filled with life, only this time it was under very different circumstances.

After Benjamin's death in 1886, Helen Edwards continued to be surrounded by friends and family. She is pictured with her daughter, Helen Edwards Condell, about 1900.

Edwards Place

Chapter Four

The Lincolns

AND EDWARDS PLACE

THERE IS A COMMON MISPERCEPTION that Abraham and Mary Lincoln were married at Edwards Place, but this is not the case. Lincoln actually called on Mary Todd at the home of her brother-in-law, Ninian W. Edwards, and married her there in 1842. That house used to stand on South Second Street before it was torn down in 1917 to make way for the Illinois Secretary of State's Building.

The Edwards Place that survives today was the home of Ninian's brother, Benjamin. And while it might not be the place where Lincoln courted Mary Todd, it does have its own ties to Abraham and Mary Lincoln.

Mary Todd was one of the first people that Benjamin and Helen Edwards met when they arrived in Springfield on January 4, 1840. Ninian had invited the new arrivals to stay with him until their own house was ready. "How quickly my fears were dispersed by the cordial welcome we received from all of the family," Helen later recalled. This family included Ninian and Elizabeth Edwards, their two children, and Mary Todd, Elizabeth's sister, who was on an extended visit from Lexington, Kentucky. Helen remembered that meeting well: "She greeted me with such warmth of manner… saying she knew we would be great friends. This bond of friendship was continued to the end of her life."

Benjamin and Helen continued to see Mary socially, even after they moved into their first house at the corner of Fourth and Monroe. Their house was not far from Ninian's, and it was also across the street from the Second Presbyterian Church, where the state senate was meeting until construction on the new state house was complete. As a result, the young people of the town often rendezvoused at Benjamin and Helen's house. Helen remembered that the other girls would "tease Mary about her 'tall beau,'" but Mary "would give them no satisfaction, neither affirming nor denying the report of her engagement to Mr. Lincoln." Privately, Helen thought that Mary was more interested in Stephen A. Douglas than Abraham Lincoln.

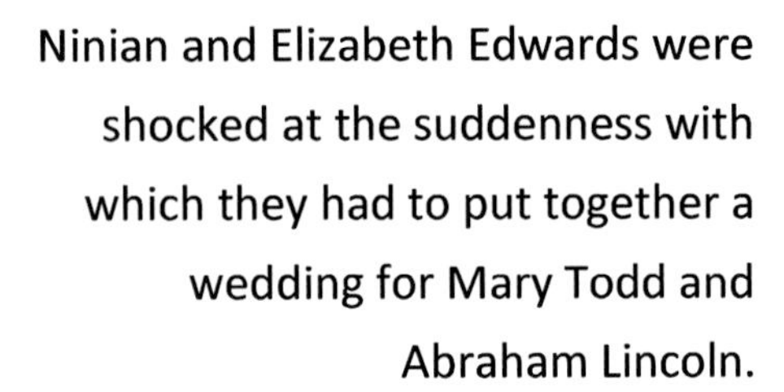

Ninian and Elizabeth Edwards were shocked at the suddenness with which they had to put together a wedding for Mary Todd and Abraham Lincoln.

Both Benjamin and Helen Edwards were surprised when Ninian came to their house early one morning and asked them to come over that evening. When Helen asked what was going on, Ninian replied, "We are going to have a wedding. I met Mr. Lincoln a while ago and he told me that he and Mary were going to be married this evening." It seems that Mary and Lincoln had been meeting in secret at the home of their mutual friend Simeon Francis, where they had conceived their plan to be married. Elizabeth, Mary's sister, was devastated that Mary had not confided in her, and frantic at the thought of pulling together a wedding on such short notice. According to Helen,

> Mrs Edwards told me afterward what a shock the news was to her & how hurt she had been at Mary's want of confidence in her. She said that after she was composed enough to see Mary & talk with her about it, she seemed very much disinclined to say anything of it, only, when she said "Mary, you have not given me much time to prepare much of a wedding entertainment for our friends. I shall have to send to old Dickey (the only bakery in town) for some ginger bread & beer," jokingly, Mary with an

indignant toss of her head said "Well that is good enough for plebians I suppose." This word, it seems, Mr Edwards in his very early acquaintance with Mr Lincoln had used in giving his opinion of Mr L & Mary had not forgotten it.

Despite the short notice, Elizabeth was able to pull together an elegant, if simple, wedding supper. Benjamin and Helen Edwards were among the small number of guests who gathered in Ninian's parlor on the rainy evening of Friday, November 4, 1842 to watch the Lincolns exchange their vows. Helen remembered the wedding as "what might be called a pretty one, simple, yet impressive." She added that, at the time, there was nothing remarkable about this wedding between an ordinary Springfield man and woman, "but if we could have had even the imagination of a thought of what the future had in store for Mr. Lincoln the most trifling incident of that event doubtless would have been impressed upon memory as with the point of a diamond."

Ninian Edwards's home and parlor on South Second Street, where the Lincolns were married. This house was razed in 1917 to make way for the Secretary of State's building.

Today the Springfield Art Association owns the mahogany-veneered, horsehair-upholstered sofa which once belonged to Ninian and Elizabeth Edwards. Dubbed the "courting couch," this sofa was in the Edwardses' parlor when young Mary Todd lived with them prior to her marriage. A handwritten note from a granddaughter of Ninian and Elizabeth Edwards states that the sofa "was one of a pair that stood in the drawing room in the days when Abraham Lincoln was calling there to court Miss Mary Todd. It was there in the double parlors on the night that he was married there to Miss Todd." This sofa was restored by The Conservation Center in 2014 thanks to the generosity of the Abraham Lincoln Bicentennial Commission, the Abraham Lincoln Association, The Prairie Eye & Lasik Center, and 195 individual donors. It holds a place of honor in the newly-restored front parlor of Edwards Place.

The crown jewel of Edwards Place's decorative arts collection is the "courting couch" where Abraham Lincoln and Mary Todd sat together during their courtship.
Photos courtesy of The Conservation Center in Chicago, IL.

Abraham Lincoln's marriage to Mary Todd made him a "connection" by marriage to Benjamin Edwards. To modern eyes, they were only very distantly related: Lincoln's wife's sister was married to Benjamin's brother. Yet kinship connections mattered in early Springfield, and everyone knew who was related. In Lincoln's view, according to his friend David Davis, "Ben was in the family." This being the case, they would cross paths at family gatherings. In 1855, for example, Mary Lincoln's cousin-in-law Mary Stuart wrote: "Last evening...we were invited to a little family gathering at Dr. Wallace's. When arrived we found the family extended, enclosing some fifty or sixty." Both the Edwardses and Lincolns were part of that extended family, and both were likely there.

In Lincoln's view, according to his friend David Davis, "Ben was in the family."

The Edwardses and Lincolns also moved in the same social circles and were almost certainly guests at each other's houses. Both families were known to host parties during the winter when the legislature was in session, Springfield's high social season. Among the invitations received by Springfield's prominent families in February of 1857 was one in Benjamin's hand that read "Mr & Mrs. B. S. Edwards will be pleased to see you on Wedn: Eve. Feb. 4 1857 at 8 o'clock" and one in Lincoln's hand that read "Mr. & Mrs. Lincoln will be pleased to see you Thursday evening Feb. 5. at 8. o'clock." The Edwardses and Lincolns likely went to each other's parties; a few weeks later Mary Lincoln wrote to her sister, "Within the last three weeks, there has been a party, almost every night." The Edwards family was also known for extending

hospitality to Benjamin's colleagues of the bench and bar. On February 5, 1858, attorney Orville H. Browning noted in his diary that he spent the evening "At B. S. Edwards to supper with the Judges and Lawyers." Abraham Lincoln was likely in attendance as well.

As attorneys, Benjamin Edwards and Abraham Lincoln were professional colleagues in addition to being in-laws and personal friends. They met in the courtroom on more than 400 occasions, either as co-counsel or opposing attorneys, and both men traveled the Eighth Judicial Circuit. One of their most high-profile cases was People v. Anderson & Anderson, which went to trial during the fall of 1856. Edwards and Lincoln defended Jane Anderson and her nephew by marriage, Theodore, who were accused of murdering Jane's husband, George. Jane and Theodore were suspected of being romantically involved, and the newspapers were filled with gory and salacious details from the trial. Edwards and Lincoln were successful in getting the defendants acquitted.

Benjamin Edwards and Abraham Lincoln were professional colleagues as well as personal friends. *Right:* The Sangamon County Courthouse, where Lincoln and Edwards served on the defense team during a scandalous murder trial.

For many years, Benjamin Edwards and Abraham Lincoln were political allies as well. Both men were Whigs from the 1840s until the mid-1850s. However, when the Whig party dissolved in the mid-1850s, they found themselves on opposite sides of the political aisle. Lincoln cast his lot with the Republicans, whom he felt offered the best hope of stopping the spread of slavery. Edwards, though not pro-slavery, nevertheless felt that the Abolitionist wing of the Republican party was too radical and became a Democrat. During the 1858 contest for Senate, Edwards supported Stephen A. Douglas over his old friend and in-law Abraham Lincoln. Edwards went so far as to host a huge political rally for Douglas on the grounds of Edwards Place on July 17, 1858. More than five thousand people attended, including several carriages full of ladies. The *Illinois State Register* reported that, in addition to cannons and bands of music, "the grove was gaily decorated with national flags, with significant mottoes." That same evening, Lincoln addressed his own followers with a speech at the State House.

Benjamin Edwards felt that Abraham Lincoln lacked the qualifications for higher office. He backed Stephen A. Douglas for Senate in 1858 and President in 1860.

Two years later, the Edwardses were surprised by Lincoln's nomination for President; as Helen said, "while respecting him as a most exemplary man it did not seem to me he was fitted for the position." But, she added, "time proved how mistaken I was." As he had two years earlier, Benjamin campaigned vigorously for the Little Giant. His opposition of Abraham Lincoln didn't sit well with his fellow congregants at the Second Presbyterian Church, most of whom were intensely loyal to Lincoln and the Union. Feelings grew bitter for the Edwards family at their church for a few years, until finally they moved to the First Presbyterian Church. Mercy Conkling described the switch in a letter to her son dated June 25, 1862: "Mr. Edwards, whom you recollect talked of changing his church connection, after the last election, is again excited to the same uncalled for step, and yesterday left the Church with his family, thereafter to attend the 1st Church. Poor man! Politics I fear will prove a terrible snare to his soul. He has left a church against whom his only charge is that the large majority of its members are opposed to him in political opinions."

Benjamin and Helen Edwards last saw Abraham Lincoln at the Great Western Rail Depot just before he boarded the train for Washington D.C.

The Edwardses saw little of the Lincolns after Lincoln was elected President of the United States. Helen recalls that the last time she saw Mary Lincoln was at a small party at the home of Dr. William Jayne. Helen congratulated Mary on the election and said "Mary, you were wise, but I used to think Mr. Douglas would be your choice." Mary replied emphatically, "No, I liked him well enough, but that was all." The last time Helen saw Abraham Lincoln was at the train depot, just before he departed for Washington D.C. "He was standing at the ticket office surrounded by a group of his friends whom he left to come over and greet us...Other friends claimed him, and we said good bye never to meet again," Helen recalled.

The Edwards family grieved when they learned of Lincoln's assassination. "His death...was a terrible shock to us all who were his warm personal friends," Helen said. When Lincoln's body came back to Springfield for interment, the Edwards family's house was filled with visitors, some of them even sleeping on cots on the library. The funeral procession passed by Edwards Place, and the Edwardses put out refreshments for the mourners as they made their way to Oak Ridge Cemetery. The Edwards family continued to think warmly of Lincoln, both as a friend and as a President. At the very end of her life, Helen spoke glowingly of the "crown of glory" Lincoln had earned, declaring "his reign was short but the results, the effect, will live forever and forever."

E PLURIBUS UNUM
Died

Edwards Place

Chapter Five

The Art Association
TAKES OVER

Historic Edwards Place—rendezvous in Springfield's earlier day of Lincoln and of other political and social personages who in point of years succeeded him—will pass this week into another epoch of existence. This time, the mission will be art.
Illinois State Journal, February 22, 1914

IN 1909, the same year that Helen Edwards died, eight local women came together to form the Amateur Art Study Club under the leadership of Georgia Miner, who became its first president. Their intent was to create an atmosphere in Springfield which was conducive to the study and appreciation of art, to foster technical development of local artists, and to instill into its students a love of the beautiful.

Each month the club met at the home of one of its members. Typical meetings consisted of refreshments, a musical presentation, and a lecture presented by the chairman of one of the club's departments: Art History, Nature Work, Designing, Craft Work, Manual Training, Wood Carving, Conventional China Painting, Naturalistic China Painting, Painting in Oil and Water Color, Work in Crayon and Pastel, Pottery, Art Needle Work, and Photography. Vachel Lindsay served as honorary chairman of the Art History Department.

Interest in the Amateur Art Study Club grew rapidly. By 1913 its membership had expanded to nearly one hundred people, and the need for a dedicated meeting place became more apparent. One of its co-founders, Elizabeth Capps, saw the now-vacant Edwards Place as a possibility for the home of the club. Capps approached Alice Edwards Ferguson and asked permission to rent a room within the home. As Elizabeth's daughter recalled, her mother was "terrified,…but she was so bursting with enthusiasm & sincerity – Mrs. Ferguson began to catch the 'bug.'" Alice first offered to let the Club use a room rent-free. A few days later, Alice called Elizabeth and said 'Mrs. Capps I'm going to let the Art Club use all the building and free of rent.'" Elizabeth was so earnest and enthusiastic in her appreciation that

Elizabeth Capps and Georgia Miner, founding members of the Springfield Amateur Art Study club.

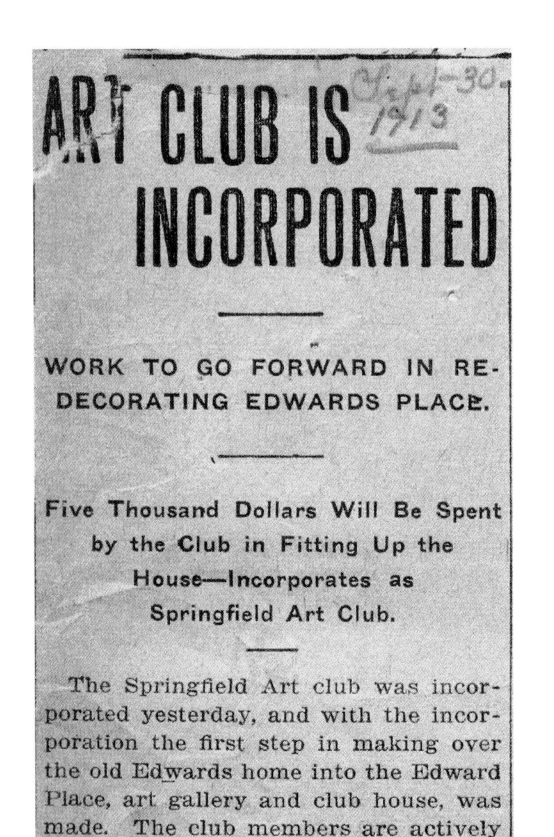

ART CLUB IS INCORPORATED

WORK TO GO FORWARD IN RE-DECORATING EDWARDS PLACE.

Five Thousand Dollars Will Be Spent by the Club in Fitting Up the House—Incorporates as Springfield Art Club.

The Springfield Art club was incorporated yesterday, and with the incorporation the first step in making over the old Edwards home into the Edward Place, art gallery and club house, was made. The club members are actively planning ways and means to raise the $5,000 which is considered necessary to

Alice finally told her "I believe I would like to give [Edwards Place] to the Art Club and make them a deed."

On September 28, 1913, the Springfield Art Club secured a charter from the State of Illinois and became officially incorporated. Shortly thereafter the deed to Edwards Place was formally presented to the Art Club at a banquet luncheon hosted by Governor Richard Yates. Alice presented the deed, saying, "I could not bear to have the old home go into other hands, and yet I did not want the beautiful place to stand idle; like an inspiration it came to me to give it to the Art Club for the young people of Springfield."

During the winter of 1913-1914, members of the newly-minted Springfield Art Association rolled up their sleeves and began the process of transforming a slightly run-down private residence into a modern art gallery. Elizabeth Capps's daughter recalled, "Mother & various club members solicited help from business firms, lumber companies, electricians, etc. And how the members pitched in, cleaning, scrubbing painting. Removing old wall papers. I worked like a slave as did dozens of others." By February, 1914, the local newspaper reported that "the house is repaired, partly repainted and papered, and an adequate heating plant installed, and some of the rooms are furnished. Electric lighting is provided throughout."

Edwards Place in its new role as headquarters of the Springfield Art Association, c. 1915.

Their goal was to have Edwards Place up and running as a gallery by late February, when their first major exhibition was scheduled to open. Shortly before opening day, Elizabeth Capps began to worry that the old floors would not support the weight of the hundreds of visitors they were expecting. When two carpenters examined the house, according to Elizabeth, "they reported to me that the Building was strong as the day it was built all the heavy pieces were oak and walnut. I saw them and they looked like new lumber."

The inaugural exhibition featured work by the up-and-coming young American artist C. Arnold Slade. More than 1,000 people attended the opening reception on February 26, 1914; as the local newspaper reported, "They went to see the creations of oil and water already on exhibition, and to familiarize themselves with the attractive interior of the old homestead which from now on shall be the rendezvous of all from this section whose interests lie in things artistic."

Next page: The dining and sitting rooms of Edwards Place as they appeared in the 1910s, when they were used as reception and meeting rooms.

Fragments of the Art Association's forest green wallpaper were found during the restoration process, as were electrical sockets installed in 1914 to provide gallery lighting.

Previous page: The upstairs bedrooms of Edwards Place were used as studios for art classes.

Inside, visitors stepped into the long hall and admired the transformation. To the left of the hall they found the "club rooms," consisting of a reception room painted in blue and white, the dining room, and a reading room beyond (known today as the sitting room, dining room, and archaeology room). On the right side of the hall, the adjoining parlors served as the exhibition space. These gallery rooms were papered in forest green ("a prettier background for pictures could scarcely be imagined," remarked the *Illinois State Journal*) and "cunningly lighted" to show the artwork to the best possible advantage. (Evidence of this green wallpaper and electrical work were discovered during the course of restoration work in Edwards Place.) The newspaper explained that "one of the rooms will be dedicated to instructional and school work, one will be filled with relics, and the last will be given over to the recognized pictures." Upstairs, two bedrooms were slated to display artwork from the public schools, and several more set aside to be rented as studios.

In its new role as an art gallery, Edwards Place was constantly bustling with activity. It aspired to be to Springfield what the Art Institute is to Chicago, and in many ways, it succeeded: many of the leading names in American art could be found at Edwards Place in the Art Association's early days. Just as it had as the Amateur Art Study Club, the Art Association hosted monthly lectures on topics that varied from weaving to sculpture to daguerreotypes to art appreciation. Now, however, it was often able to attract leading artists such as Pauline Palmer, Lorado Taft, Jens Jenson and Gutzon Borglum to deliver the talks. Admission to the lectures was free to members and twenty-five cents to nonmembers. Starting with the Slade exhibit in February of 1914, the Art Association commenced an ambitious schedule of exhibitions which featured some of the nation's most prominent artists. In its first few years alone, the Art

Association showed works by luminaries such as James Abbot McNeill Whistler, Winslow Homer, Dawson Dawson-Watson, and Childe Hassam, as well as hosted travelling exhibitions assembled by national arts groups such as the American Federation of Arts, the National Society of Etchers, and the New York Watercolor Society.

The Art Association's development was shepherded and supported by Alice Edwards Ferguson, who served as a sort of patron saint to the organization in its early years. A woman of naturally refined tastes and an appreciation for culture, she wholeheartedly endorsed the Art Association's mission of uplifting society through the exposure to the beautiful. Her gift of Edwards Place was just the beginning of her generosity to the Art Association: she also donated original family objects to furnish Edwards Place; contributed pieces of art from her personal collection as well as money for the purchase of artwork; made monetary donations when finances were tight; and gave her time and energy at countless events. When she died, the first president of the Art Association wrote in a memorial, "The harmony and general good will which always existed between her and the members of the Art Association was as remarkable as it was beautiful. She gave without exacting and in return they worked without asking." Her death was, to the Art Association, an "irretrievable loss."

Child of Spain by Pauline Palmer, donated to the Art Association by Alice Edwards Ferguson.

The harmony and good will which always existed between Alice Edwards Ferguson and the members of the Art Association was as remarkable as it was beautiful...

WALLACE DE WOLF, noted American artist, will furnish and decorate the north room of the galleries of Edwards place in memory of his wife. The late Mrs. DeWolf was Miss Mary Rae, daughter of Mrs. Julia Ridgely Rae, formerly of this city.

Illinois State Register,

June 8, 1917.

False walls, added in the children's parlor to create the DeWolf Memorial Gallery in 1917, were removed during the 2014 restoration.

As the headquarters of the Springfield Art Association, Edwards Place continued to evolve in response to changing needs and circumstances. After the death of his wife in 1915, wealthy Chicago businessman and amateur artist Wallace DeWolf underwrote the creation of the DeWolf Memorial Gallery in the northernmost of the four adjoining parlors. This gallery, dedicated exclusively to DeWolf's own artwork, was opened to the public on September 20, 1917. By the 21st century, no one recalled that this Memorial Gallery had ever existed in Edwards Place. During the course of restoration, however, it was discovered that the walls in the fourth parlor were furred out by six inches all the way around. This new wall, covered with canvas, became a much sturdier surface on which to hang artwork. Although it was exciting to find evidence of this long-forgotten, nearly century-old gallery, the false walls were ultimately removed to restore the room to its original 19th century profile.

By the 1930s, it became apparent that the Art Association needed more space than Edwards Place could provide. After several years of planning and fundraising, a new, fireproof gallery was constructed adjacent to the historic house in 1937. With the Gallery of Art no longer occupying the parlors, the decision was made to return Edwards Place to its pre-Civil War appearance. These rooms were fitted with period-appropriate drapery, wallpaper, and carpeting, and augmented by donations of nineteenth century furniture which came in from Edwards family descendants as well as descendants of several other, prominent Springfield families. The first two parlors were restored in 1938, and the dining room, sitting room, and small dining room were completed in 1944. The authentically-appointed formal parlors were featured in the July, 1945 issue of *The Magazine Antiques.*

EDWARDS PLACE

In Abraham Lincoln's Springfield

By VIRGINIA SINCLAIR CATRON
and MARY MASTERS

EDWARDS PLACE IS THE OLDEST HOUSE on its own grounds in Springfield, Illinois, and for a hundred and twelve years has been dominant in the cultural life of the town. From 1833 to 1909 it was a gracious private home. Since 1913 it has been the home of the Springfield Art Association, with its fine gallery and flourishing art school. The house stands in its original grove of elms and maples on North Fifth Street, where its widely overhanging cornice, a spacious piazza with Corinthian columns, and fanciful cupola recall the Victorian era of Abraham Lincoln's town.

Built in 1833, and well and sturdily of fine wood, the original part of the house known as Edwards Place was erected by Doctor Thomas Houghan. It then stood outside the limits of the town of 1,200, surrounded by its own fourteen acres of ground and bordered by the virgin prairie.

Mrs. Benjamin S. Edwards, who had come to Springfield as a bride of four months in January 1840, moved to this home in the summer of 1843, with her husband and infant daughter, Helen, when Mr. Edwards purchased the estate from Doctor Houghan. She said of it many years afterward: "At first it was lonely indeed. There was not a house in sight except a little log school house." Benjamin S. Edwards was a prominent and successful lawyer, a judge, the youngest son of Ninian Edwards, governor of the territory, and afterwards third governor (*1826-1830*) of the State of Illinois. He was Yale University's first graduate from Illinois and he married his college sweetheart, Helen K. Dodge, in New Haven in 1839. During

EDWARDS PLACE
In Abraham Lincoln's Springfield
By VIRGINIA SINCLAIR CATRON
and MARY MASTERS

The restored first floor of Edwards Place was featured in the July, 1945 issue of *The Magazine Antiques.*

A new, fireproof gallery was constructed adjacent to Edwards Place in 1937.

As the Art Association continued to grow, so did its campus. The Condell Art Studio was built in 1949 and enlarged in 1964, the Gallery of Art was expanded in 1968, and office space was constructed in 1978-1980. These changes fundamentally changed the relationship between Edwards Place and the Art Association. In the beginning, Edwards Place *was* the Springfield Art Association; the organization and its headquarters were so closely linked in the public's mind that the two names were used interchangeably and synonymously. As late as the 1960s, art classes were still being held in the bedrooms of Edwards Place, prompting many a fond memory of painting on the walls and sliding down the bannisters. As classes and exhibits moved into their own dedicated spaces, however, the role of Edwards Place within the Art Association had to be reassessed and redefined.

Previous page: The parlors of Edwards Place, restored in the 1940s, were used for Art Association meetings and events.

The upstairs bedrooms of Edwards Place were being used for children's art classes as late as the 1960s.

The Springfield Art Association's mission includes a mandate to preserve Edwards Place, and the organization decided to honor that by opening the house to the community as a museum. Throughout the next several decades, the Art Association took several important steps to preserve and promote the historic house. In 1969, Edwards Place was listed on the National Register of Historic Places. In the 1970s, the first of several formal inventories and appraisals of the permanent collection of art and artifacts took place. Special events and tours highlighting life in 19th century-era Springfield are offered on a regular basis.

However, there was more work to be done. Until recently Edwards Place, lacked the benefit of a comprehensive restoration plan, a thorough understanding of the house's history and evolution, and an interpretive plan to shape the visitors experience. As a result, the significance of Edwards Place had lately been overlooked by locals and visitors alike.

Within the past several years, the Art Association has taken steps to integrate Edwards place within the fabric of the community. Now, as momentum and excitement are building around Edwards Place and all it has to offer, the Art Association has implemented an ambitious plan to undertake a full-scale restoration of the stately mansion to its mid-19th century appearance.

Restoration of Edwards Place will allow the Springfield Art Association to continue to bring history to life for our community and visitors alike.

Edwards Place

Chapter Six

Restoration Work

BEGINS AT EDWARDS PLACE

THERE IS NO PLACE LIKE EDWARDS PLACE. As the oldest surviving house in Springfield, it has deep architectural significance. As a repository of storied local antiques, it has an invaluable collection of decorative arts and artifacts. And as the social center for Illinois's 19th century politicians, its parlors echo with the footsteps of every leading light in our state's history, from Abraham Lincoln to Ulysses S. Grant. Edwards Place may be owned and operated by the Springfield Art Association, but its history and significance belong to the entire community. Edwards Place is a lens through which we can observe the past and, in so doing, glimpse the people, circumstances, and values that made us who we are today.

It was with the community in mind that the Springfield Art Association decided to undertake a full-scale restoration of Edwards Place to its c. 1857 appearance. Its vision is to offer the community a historically-accurate window into one of the most significant time periods in our state's history, which will allow visitors to immerse themselves in the culture of the mid-19th century.

The first steps were taken in 2009, when the Art Association applied for and was awarded a grant from the Jeffris Family Foundation to match the cost of a Decorative Arts Analysis. In 2010 funds from that grant were used to hire the firm of Sullivan Preservation of Chicago to undertake an Interior Finishes and Furnishings Plan, which was completed in June of 2011. This Plan laid out recommendations for furniture conservation, wallpaper, floor coverings, window treatments and wood graining to restore the interior to an appearance appropriate to a prosperous family in the mid-19th century.

With a roadmap in hand, the last hurdle to restoration was also the largest: raising the necessary funds to underwrite the work. The price tag of $850,000 was daunting. The Art Association decided to restore the house in three

Next page: The dining room was restored in 2012-13 at a cost of $36,000.

phases: first the dining room as a "test run" and showpiece, then the first floor, and finally the second floor. Work in the dining room would begin the following summer, and the first floor would be completed once the necessary $500,000 was in hand. Fundraising for the second floor would commence when the first floor was finished. With that goal in mind, the Art Association began.

Restoration began on the dining room in June, 2012. Working from the Sullivan plan, the room received structural repairs to the plaster and updated electrical systems, faux walnut graining on the trim, the installation of new wallpaper and carpeting; a painted plaster ceiling medallion and window cornice, and the restoration and rewiring of the original 1850s chandelier. The total cost to restore the dining room was $36,000. The bulk of the funds were raised as a "fund-a-project" at the 2011 Beaux Arts Ball, with private donations and the Springfield Art Association's general operating funds supplying the balance. Restoring the dining room proved to be excellent preparation for tackling the restoration of the rest of the house.

The dining room before and during the restoration process.

Next page: The formal parlor, sitting room, library, and children's parlor prior to restoration.

It also was an excellent jumpstart to the Art Association's fundraising campaign. When the dining room reopened to the public, its stunning appearance energized donors to contribute to the restoration fund. Fundraising efforts were boosted significantly by a challenge grant awarded by the Jeffris Family Foundation in the amount of $150,000, to be claimed when the Springfield Art Association matched it with $300,000. This milestone was reached late in 2013, more than two years ahead of schedule. The generosity of the Jeffris Family Foundation and many donors in reaching the fundraising goal meant that restoration of the first floor could begin in 2014.

On April 26, 2014, the doors were closed and work began in earnest to clear out the house in advance of restoration. Smaller pieces of furniture and objets d'art went upstairs into the bedrooms, while larger pieces of furniture were moved into the dining room for safekeeping. By May 1, 2014, the first floor was empty, and restoration work was set to begin. For the next ten months, Edwards Place was in the hands of a team of incredibly talented and dedicated professionals who transformed it from a slightly shabby old house to a breathtaking slice of the 19th century.

Below: Case furniture was sealed in the dining room for safekeeping, while chairs, paintings, and smaller items were stored upstairs.

Project Manager: CJP ARCHITECTS

As Project Manager of the Edwards Place restoration, Charles Joseph Pell, AIA, served as the "man behind the curtain," overseeing the process to make sure everything ran smoothly, on time, and on budget. Pell steered the Art Association through the process of soliciting bids from contractors. Once the bids were in, he did the delicate dance of hiring the best people at the most reasonable prices. Pell also served as the Art Association's liaison with the Jeffris Family Foundation by making sure that the SAA's plans and contractors were in accordance with the Foundation's guidelines.

Pell was a common fixture at Edwards Place during the restoration process, checking on progress, nudging contractors, and ensuring that plans were being followed and goals were being met. Pell deftly handled unforeseen issues as they arose, such as the need to level the ceiling in the children's parlor, arranging for the necessary structural repairs without sacrificing time or the budget. When the main staircase was found to be sagging, Pell designed a plan for shoring it up, resulting in stairs that are now as solid as they day they were installed.

Pell obtained his Bachelor of Architecture from the University of Arkansas and lived and worked in Washington, DC before returning to Springfield and establishing his practice in 1993. His award-winning firm has experience that is broad and abilities that are well-proven. Since its founding, CJP Architects has completed many diverse projects for various State of Illinois agencies, a new multi-purpose addition to the Washington Park Botanical Garden, a renovation of Butler Elementary School for District 186, numerous private residences, and projects at the Illinois Capitol for the Office of the Architect of the Capitol, among others.

Next page: Project Manager Charles Pell of CJP Architects inspects work on the main staircase, for which he designed structural repairs.

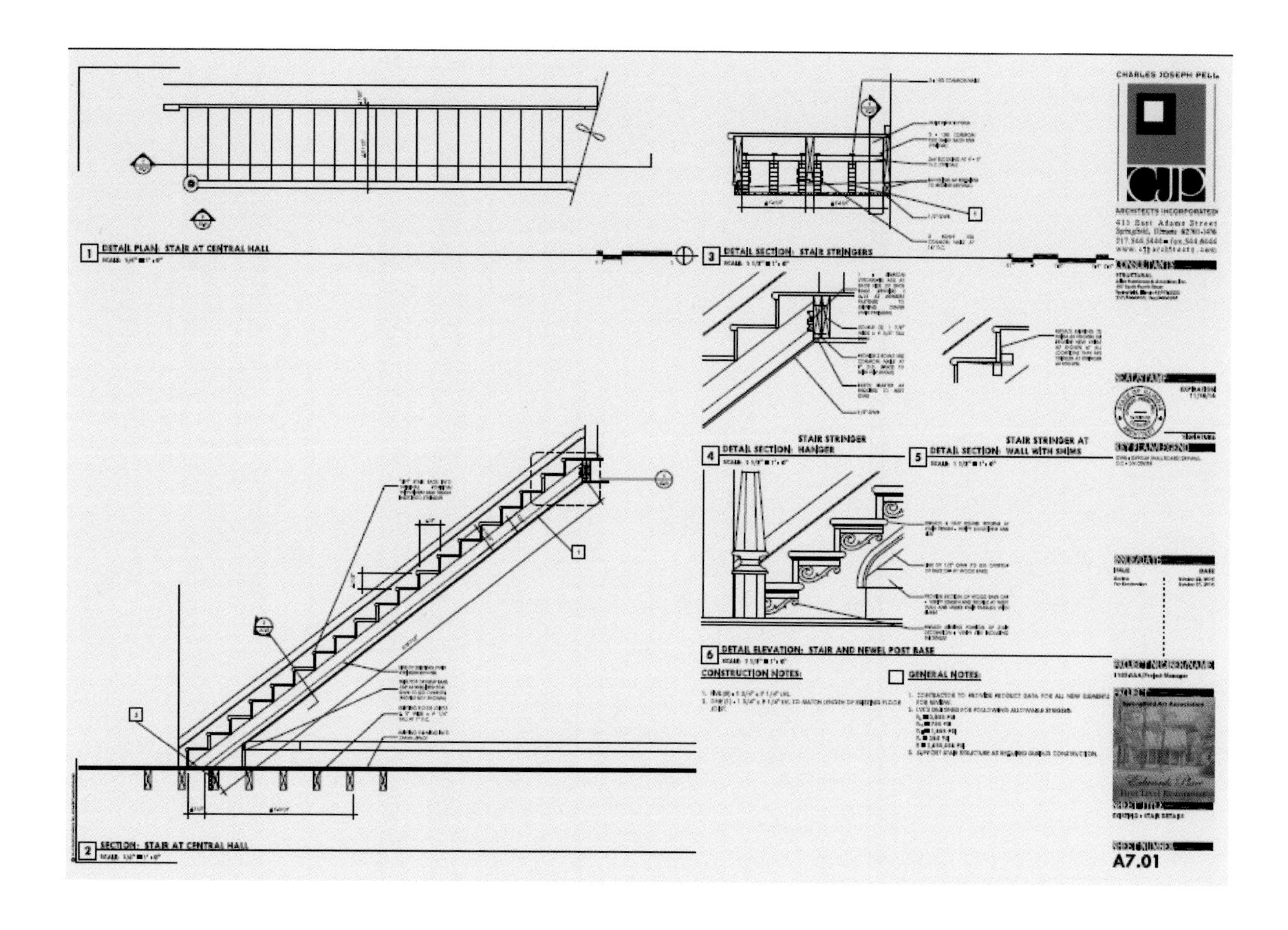
CHARLES JOSEPH PELL
ARCHITECTS INCORPORATED
1 DETAIL PLAN: STAIR AT CENTRAL HALL
3 DETAIL SECTION: STAIR STRINGERS
CONSULTANTS
STAIR STRINGER
4 DETAIL SECTION: HANGER
STAIR STRINGER AT
5 DETAIL SECTION: WALL WITH SHIMS
6 DETAIL ELEVATION: STAIR AND NEWEL POST BASE
CONSTRUCTION NOTES:
GENERAL NOTES:
2 SECTION: STAIR AT CENTRAL HALL
A7.01

Electrical Work: MANSFIELD ELECTRIC COMPANY

Led by foreman R. Travis Savage, the team from Mansfield Electric updated the wiring, refurbished the chandeliers, and installed new fixtures in Edwards Place.

Before the Springfield Art Association could think about putting beautifully-crafted, historically-accurate wallpaper on the walls, it first needed to deal with an issue inside the walls: the electrical wiring. The most recent electrical updates in the house dated to the Second World War. In many places, the wiring hadn't been touched since it was installed by the Art Association in 1914. It was clear that the entire first floor would need an electrical upgrade, and that this process would need to take place before any finishes could be applied.

The Art Association turned to Mansfield Electric Company for its electrical needs. Founded in 1949, Mansfield has a long history of exceptional service in the Springfield area. Its reputation is rooted in a commitment to solid management, skilled labor, innovative cost control, and adaptability to changing technology. Mansfield's previous clients include the Vachel Lindsay Home State Historic Site, and the Abraham Lincoln Presidential Library. Mansfield also updated the wiring in the Edwards Place dining room in 2012.

Electrical work began on the first floor of Edwards Place during the summer of 2014. Led by foreman R. Travis Savage, the crew from Mansfield channeled into the plaster to access the wiring. They found cloth-covered wires dating to the 1950s. These were replaced with modern wires, and the outlets were upgraded from two-prong receptacles to three-prong receptacles. The

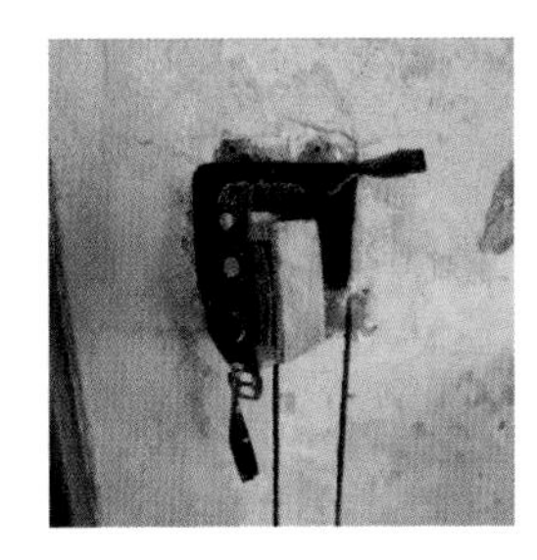

chandelier light fixtures were also rewired, and their switches upgraded to include a dimmer function. Four of these chandeliers belonged to the Edwards family and were originally installed as gas fixtures in 1857. Recessed lighting was also added to the ceilings of each room to spotlight artwork and significant artifacts in the Edwards Place collection.

Finally, Mansfield Electric updated the lighting in the two windows on the east side of the house in the front parlors. These windows used to look out onto the Edwardses' formal gardens. When the adjacent Gallery of Art was expanded in 1967, however, the windows were completely blocked by the new construction and fitted with fluorescent light fixtures. Mansfield replaced outdated fixtures and replaced them with strips of LED-lighting attached to a dimmer switch to better simulate natural light. The result is an historic house suffused with soft, warm light, drawing people in just as the gaslights did a century and a half ago.

Updated lighting brought warmth and brightness to Edwards Place without compromising its historic character.

Since 1913
EVANS
CONSTRUCTION CO.

Next page: Evans' extensive work in the children's parlor included repairing and reinstalling the trim around the doorway and installing new trim around the large window.

Construction Work: EVANS CONSTRUCTION COMPANY

The restoration of Edwards Place was conceived as a rehabilitation of interior finishes, but inevitably, in a project of this scope, structural problems turned up that needed repair. The Springfield Art Association turned to Evans Construction Company to handle these repairs to ensure that the house was structurally sound prior to receiving new wallpaper and carpeting.

Much of Evans' work centered around the children's parlor. Their first task was addressing the drooping ceiling. An exploratory hole in the ceiling revealed that the cause of this trouble dated all the way back to 1857. That year, the Edwards family built a new kitchen and removed the cooking fireplace from this room, which had been their old kitchen. When they did so, the joist that used to but up against the chimney was left unsupported, eventually causing the ceiling to sag. Evans reinforced this joist and patched the hole, leaving an even ceiling.

The children's parlor also had issues that presented themselves when the false walls were removed. The original profile of the room was revealed to include a doorway out to the porch. The doorway itself was blocked up in the 1970s, but the trim survived. Evans was able to retrofit a door from elsewhere in the house to fit into the trim, restoring the illusion of an exit onto the porch. Evans also had replacement trim milled and installed to patch a gap in the baseboard created by yet another doorway. This one, on the north wall, was installed in 1857 after the chimney was removed and bricked up sometime in the late 19th century. Finally, Evans reinforced the large picture window and had it fitted with custom-milled trim. Because this window obviously dates to the 20th century, the new trim was milled to complement the existing woodwork rather than to mimic it exactly.

Evans construction replaced joists in the ceiling of the children's parlor to eliminate its pronounced sag.

Next page: The main staircase, stabilized and restored.

Cosmetic and structural repairs were also needed on the main stairs. Evans removed a small closet, installed under the stairs in 1930, to restore the hallway to its mid-19th century appearance. In an effort to stabilize the once again free-floating staircase, Evans installed seven large support beams, each capable of handling two million pounds of pressure per square inch.

In addition to these major projects, Evans had replacement woodwork milled and installed wherever it was missing on the first floor, removed tack strips from the old carpet, and removed windows in the front parlor to allow access for improved lighting. The result of all their effort is a house that is structurally sound enough to withstand the next 180 years.

Evans demolished the c. 1930s closet beneath the stairs and stabilized the staircase.

Plaster Repair, Wallpaper Installation, Wood Refinishing, and Painting:

FRITSCH CUSTOM FINISHES

Minimal to moderate plaster repair was required in the sitting room (*top*), hallway (*middle*) and formal parlors (*bottom*).

As one would expect in a house built in the 1830s, age had taken its toll on much of the plaster, paint, and woodwork in Edwards Place. The Springfield Art Association trusted the work of removing old wallpaper, repairing the plaster, preparing the substrate, painting the walls, refinishing the woodwork, and hanging wallpaper to Fritsch Custom Finishes.

Fritsch is one of the few firms in the area with the expertise necessary to handle the intricacies of restoring an historic house. The company was founded in 1930 by Harry Fritsch, and continues its 80+ year tradition of excellence under the leadership of C. Wendell Fritsch, Harry's grandson. Previous clients include the Dana-Thomas House and the Illinois State Capitol Building; work at the latter was praised as "fabulous" and "above and beyond all expectations."

The Springfield Art Association found this to be the case with work on Edwards Place, as well. After removing the wallpaper throughout the first floor, Fristch found the plaster in varying states of repair or disrepair. In the sitting room and hallway, where extensive plaster work had been conducted within the past 10 years, the walls needed only minimal repairs to the electrical channels and a skim coat. The walls of the parlors had been stabilized in the 1990s and, for the most part, also required only a skim coat, although the removal of the mid-twentieth-century crown molding resulted in the need for extensive patching near the ceiling.

The library and children's parlor were a different story. In the library, removal of the wallpaper exposed sheetrock installed in the 1960s. A peek beneath this sheetrock on the south wall led to the discovery of fragments of wallpaper dating to the 1850s. The Edwards Place Committee decided to remove the rest of the sheetrock in the library in the hopes of uncovering more original wallpaper. In this endeavor they were successful: enough 1850s wallpaper was recovered to make its reproduction possible. As a bonus, several fragments of a later paper were also recovered on the southwest wall. Likely installed in the late 1870s, this later paper is a mosaic of dark purple, green, and gold that would have given the library a dark and masculine feel.

Underneath this wallpaper, however, the pre-Civil-War-era plaster was crumbling. The same was true in the adjacent children's parlor, where the removal of false walls revealed plaster which had been installed in the 1830s and 1850s and had not been seen since the 1910s. In both rooms, Gerry Whalen, Mark Jones, Kenny Lamotte, and Mike Jones from Fritsch completely reworked the plaster, in many places from the lath up.

Removal of 1960s sheetrock in the library led to the discovery of wallpaper fragments dating to the 19th century under green wallpaper installed by the Art Association in 1914.

The white paper with gold accents (*left*) dates to 1857, while the darker paper (*right*) was likely installed in the late 1870s or early 1880s.

The plaster in the library, hidden under sheetrock for more than 50 years, required extensive repairs.

Removal of false walls in the children's parlor revealed plaster walls not seen for almost a century. This room, like the library, required extensive plaster work.

"Windows" were built into the plaster to reveal architectural features such as the arch , hand-riven lath, ghosts of original wallpaper, and original whitewashed brick.

In addition to simply repairing or redoing the plaster, Fritsch was able to work with the Edwards Place Committee's evolving plans to preserve architectural features within the house for public view. In the children's playroom, Fritsch left a section of 1830s, hand-riven lath exposed in the ceiling and a square of plaster bearing the ghostly imprint of its original wallpaper exposed on the wall. In the library, an original section of 1850s wallpaper was preserved on the south wall. Above it, a masonry arch was left exposed. This arch framed a door or window when the house was constructed in 1833. Its presence is a striking illustration of the way the house evolved over the decades of its occupancy. Finally, in the hallway, three windows were opened into the plaster to expose the original 1830s brick underneath. Springfield Art Association Board Member Clay Crocker designed and built a brilliant mechanism to frame these windows with doors that can be opened to reveal the brick beneath or closed to blend in with the wall. Fritsch plastered these frames into place and later wallpapered around them.

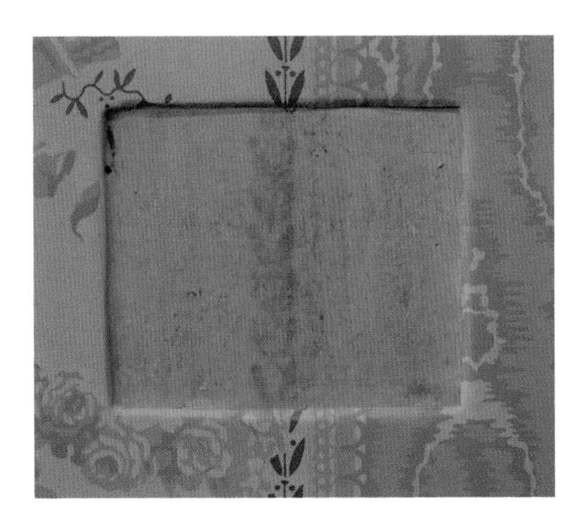

Once the plaster work was finished, the team from Fritsch drew on their extensive experience refinishing woodwork to return the stairs and walnut trim to their original beauty. Denny Gillette, Abby Styber, Jake Mahon, Tom Jennings and Ben Dodson spent countless hours patiently stripping and sanding the oak spindles and walnut handrail of the staircases, which glowed to life with the application of varnish and lacquer. In the front parlors and library, they removed more than a century of accumulated varnish and grime from the walnut trim, revealing the exquisite grain of wood that was more than likely harvested locally in the 1830s, then stained it to bring out its rich beauty. Steve Sagle completed the process by applying a spray coat of lacquer to preserve character of the newly-refinished wood for future generations.

Fritsch's team painstakingly stripped, sanded, stained, and lacquered the original walnut trim and doors to restore their natural beauty.

Bret Dalby restored the chandeliers to their original luster. Each of the seven fixtures were disassembled and their parts stripped of old paint and varnish. They were then repainted, reassembled, and sent to Mansfield Electric to be rewired. Once installed and fitted with globes, they looked just as they must have in the 1850s when the Edwards family first stood in their glow and marveled at the miracle of gas lighting.

The last project undertaken by Fritsch also had the biggest visual impact: hanging wallpaper in each of the downstairs rooms. This task required extreme care, as many of the papers were unusually fragile. It also required meticulous attention to detail to ensure that the papers' intricate patterns aligned (or staggered) correctly. Gillette, Sagle, and Robert Smith were up to the task, skillfully negotiating corners and windows while maintaining precise vertical alignment. Their hard work brought the first floor of Edwards Place to life as patterns familiar to the Edwards family once again graced the walls, ready to welcome visitors into a slice of the 19th century.

Bret Dalby dismantled, cleaned, polished, and painted all the chandeliers to return them to their original luster.

Wallpaper installation in the sitting room, front hall, formal parlors, and library.

Ed Gonet of Gonet Designs Corporation.

Faux Painting: GONET DESIGNS CORPORATION

Much of the wooden trim in Edwards Place is pine that had been painted white, but thanks to the magic of Ed Gonet's faux painting, that trim now looks like it was made of walnut and oak, just as it did when the Edwards family lived there.

Faux painting is a decorative finish that simulates materials such as marble and wood. It has been a popular decorating motif since classical times, and it experienced a resurgence during the neoclassical revival of the 18th and 19th centuries. This technique was designed to give inexpensive wood and plaster surfaces the appearance of marble or more expensive woods.

The portions of Edwards Place dating to the 1830s all contain walnut trim and woodwork. However, all the woodwork installed during the 1857 remodel of the house is pine. Pine from the northern Great Lakes became available in Illinois after railroads and the Illinois and Michigan Canal linked Springfield to Chicago in the late 1840s and 1850s. Although pine produced long, straight logs that were excellent for construction purposes, it was considered a "lesser wood," something less valuable and desirable than domestic hardwoods such as walnut and oak or exotics such as mahogany and rosewood. Many people, including the Edwards family, turned to faux painters to replicate these expensive woods.

The skill of faux painting was relatively well known in the 19th century, but now, in the 21st century, skilled artisans capable of doing this work are few and far between. The Springfield Art Association was fortunate to hire Ed Gonet, a master painter.

Gonet's process involves seven steps to achieve the accuracy and subtlety necessary to successfully simulate wood grain. His attention to detail even goes so far as to simulate varying cuts of woods. People alive during the nineteenth century were much more familiar with species and cuts of wood than we are in modern times and would have understood the visual appeal and expense of select cuts of wood.

Gonet's work began in the sitting room. This room was added to the house in 1857 and finished with pine trim. Paint analysis suggests that the pine woodwork in this room was faux-grained to resemble walnut at some point during the Edwards family's tenure and then subsequently painted white by the Art Association. Gonet employed his seven-step process to simulate a walnut grain in the sitting room, complementing his earlier work on the adjacent dining room. To achieve the flawless look of hardwood grain, Gonet first preps the wood by sanding, patching, and sanding again. He then primes the wood and often does another round of patching and sanding. One more layer of primer is added, and then the underglaze is applied using a "flogging" technique. Gonet then skillfully paints the trim to mimic the grain of the desired wood and applies a final layer of glaze to give it richness and depth.

Gonet's process includes patching, sanding, priming, flogging, graining, and glazing the wood to simulate the appearance of walnut.

Below : The trim in the servants' hallway was restored to its original, putty-gray color scheme. *Right:* Gonet discovered and recreated the original oak faux finish in the front hall.

While sanding the front hallway and stairs, Gonet discovered an original faux oak finish dating to 1857 buried under decades of accumulated varnish and grime. Oak, especially quarter-sawn oak, was expensive and highly coveted in the mid-19th century for its attractive grain pattern. The Edwards family used it in their front hallway to convey a sense of taste and refinement to their visitors. Over the course of several weeks, Gonet painstakingly recreated the oak graining on the trim and baseboards in the front hall, as well as the front door and main staircase. The results are simply spectacular.

Gonet discovered a surprise while sanding the back hallway: the trim and rear stairs were originally painted a putty gray, not faux grained as originally believed. The rear hall and stairs was the "servants" portion of the house, and the Edwards family clearly wished to draw a visual distinction between it and the main portion of the house. Although the initial work plan called for the back hallway to be faux grained, the Edwards Place Committee unanimously voted to paint the back hall gray as it was in the Edwardses' time.

On the east side of Edwards Place, the two formal parlors and the library all have walnut trim dating to the 1830s. The trim in the parlors dates to the original construction of the house in 1833, while the trim in the library dates to the construction of an addition in 1836. When the house was remodeled in 1857, however, slight alterations to these rooms resulted in the addition of small sections of pine trim. The kitchen, to the extreme north, was converted into more formal living space with the addition of pine trim milled to match the older walnut trim. Finally, large pine pocket doors were added between the children's parlor and library and the library and music room. This pine woodwork was all faux-painted walnut in 1857 to blend with the earlier walnut trim. Over the decades, many layers of varnish were applied, and the faux painting darkened to the point of being unrecognizable. Thanks to Gonet's artistry, however, the pine woodwork in the formal parlors, library, and children's playroom is now virtually indistinguishable from the walnut woodwork.

Gonet matched the color and grain of existing walnut trim in the library.

When complete, Gonet's work is indistinguishable from the wood he simulates. *Left*: faux-painted door surrounded by walnut trim. *Right:* walnut trim on the left, faux-painted trim on the right.

Wallpaper and Textile Consultants:

BELFRY HISTORIC CONSULTANTS, INC.

Just six months before restoration work was scheduled to begin on Edwards Place, the Springfield Art Association learned that not one, but two of the wallpaper suppliers specified in its Furnishing and Finishes Plan had gone out of business. Without a pattern in hand for the sitting room, parlors, library, and children's parlor, the Edwards Place Committee had to go back to the drawing board to select new patterns appropriate to the mid-19th century.

This time, the Art Association turned to Belfry Historic Consultants for assistance. Belfry has purveyed historically accurate, documented fabrics, carpeting, wallpapers, trimmings, and research since 1986. The firm specializes in high quality offerings from around the world which combine period authenticity, unmatched quality, and exceptional beauty.

With Catherine Buscemi's expert guidance, the Edwards Place Committee selected the "Edenderry" pattern by David Skinner Wallpapers for the sitting room. This informal, green striped pattern is a reproduction of an 1840s paper discovered in the Woodstock House in County Wicklow, Ireland. The Committee next chose an 1840s geometric design called "Uppark Trellis" by Hamilton Weston Wallpapers for the front and rear halls.

Belfry Historic was also worked closely with David Skinner Wallpapers to facilitate the reproduction of original fragments of wallpaper revealed in Edwards Place during the restoration process. In the library, removal of 50-year -old sheetrock led to the discovery of remnants of wallpaper first installed in 1857. A few weeks later, tiny scraps of the same paper were found in the adjoining children's parlor. Thanks to a generous grant from the Community

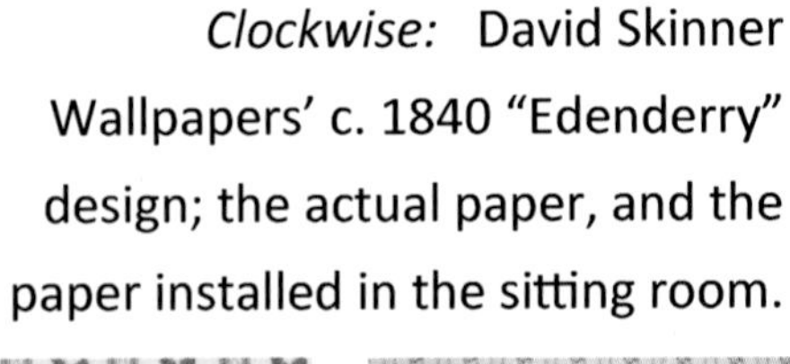

Clockwise: David Skinner Wallpapers' c. 1840 "Edenderry" design; the actual paper, and the paper installed in the sitting room.

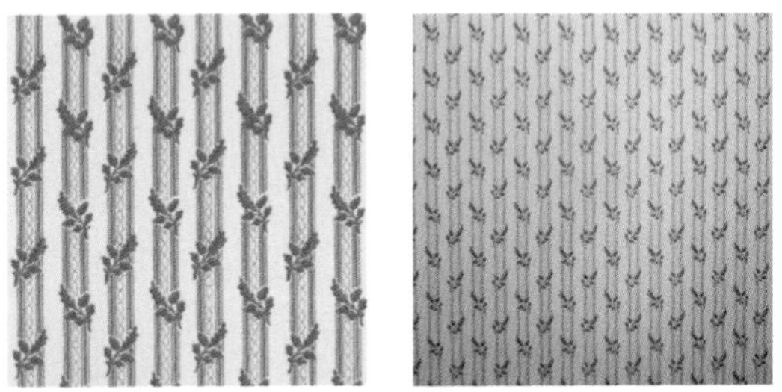

Foundation of the Land of Lincoln, the SAA was able to reproduce this pattern and install it on the walls where it originally hung.

For the parlor, the decision was made to install a reproduction of c. 1850 wallpaper found in the cellar stairway. Fragments of these papers were carefully removed from the walls and sent to Belfry Historic, who in turn forwarded them to David Skinner in Ireland. Skinner analyzed each fragment in order to reproduce the pattern and colors as accurately as possible. He determined that the parlor paper was a two-color print with a horizontal repeat of 18.5 inches, suggesting it was produced in the United States or possibly France. With a full repeat of this pattern to work with, Skinner was able to recreate exuberant white scrollwork on a beige ground with cobalt blue accents.

His task was a little more challenging with the library paper, as the fragments were smaller and the ink of the pattern had migrated almost entirely. Combining meticulous examination with archival research, Skinner determined that this paper was grounded in an satin-finish, off-white color. Its floral pattern was block-printed in two shades of gray interwoven with metallic gold/bronze accent. This paper also measured 18.5 inches across, indicating that it, too was likely of American or French origin.

Digital mockups in subtly varying colorways were sent to the Edwards Place Committee for review. Once a selection was made, Skinner printed and sent proofs, again with subtle variations. Again a selection was made, and then production of the wallpaper was under way. Although the original library paper was likely block printed and the original parlor paper was likely machine printed, Skinner employed a silk screening technique. This process, which allows for the highest-quality hand prints, employs several steps: first a stencil pattern must be created for each color to be printed, and they all must align

Clockwise: Hamilton Weston's c. 1860 "Uppark Trellis" design; the actual paper, and the paper installed in the front hall.

perfectly. Next, screens are made by coating a silk screen with a photo-sensitive emulsion, creating a large piece of film. The screen and artwork are sandwiched in a large vacuum frame and exposed to light. Areas exposed to the light become impervious; the other areas can be washed out. Finally, ink is forced through the screen stencil using a plastic-bladed squeegee. Each screen lays down one color. This means that the library paper, which has three colors, had to be printed three times with three different screens.

The results are breathtaking. Prior to the restoration process, the Springfield Art Association was unaware that any original wallpaper fragments survived from the Edwards family's residency. Now, the east half of the first floor is covered in patterns originally selected by Helen Edwards more than a century and a half ago.

Previous page: David Skinner Wallpapers was able to reproduce wallpaper for the parlor from an 1850s fragment found in a closet.

Top right: David Skinner meticulously reproduced the original 1850s pattern using a multi-step silk screen technique.

Below and right: Skinner was also able to reproduce wallpaper for the library and children's parlor. Now the reproduction hangs next to the original surviving paper in the library.

Carpet Consultant and Supplier:

THE ENGLISH WILTON COMPANY

Early in the restoration process, members of the Edwards Place Committee made the carefully-considered decision to depart from the Sullivan Furnishing and Finishes Plan's recommendations for carpeting. Ever mindful of the budget, the Committee was daunted by Sullivan's estimates and confident that a product of equal quality could be found elsewhere.

The committee discovered this high-quality, affordably-priced historic carpet at the English Wilton Company; the preeminent North American resource for the finest quality Wilton, Brussels and Axminster carpet weaves. The company's dedicated craftsmen bring together decades of experience and knowledge in historic carpet manufacturing. Their patterns are drawn from an extensive archive of 18th and 19th century designs, and the carpet is manufactured in 27" strips on the same English looms that have been in use since the 1800s. In this way, English Wilton's carpets are not "reproductions" so much as "still-in-productions."

The Springfield Art Association is deeply grateful to Dan Cooper for guiding the Committee through the process of selecting carpeting for five downstairs rooms plus the hallway. Dan's tremendous expertise is matched only by his willingness to go above and beyond for his clients. He soothed fears about the wisdom of putting two discordant patterns next to each other by assuring the Committee that this was completely acceptable by 19th century design standards. With his assistance, the Committee selected a diamond geometric red pattern for the informal sitting room, a rich green lozenge-shaped pattern for the hallway, an exuberant red and blue Rococo Revival pattern for the parlors, a bold Gothic design for the library, and a fanciful floral motif with a dark ground for the children's parlor, all appropriate to the mid-19th century appearance of Edwards Place.

The English Wilton Company's carpets are woven in 27" strips on the same looms that have been in use since the 19th century.

Dan Cooper, consultant at The English Wilton Company.

Sitting room

Hallway

Library

Front parlors

Children's parlor

The Gfroerer Rug Company of Cincinnati, Ohio has been in business since 1890.

Opposite page: Led by Bryan Gfroerer, the team from Gfroerer Rug installed carpeting in the parlors, sitting room, hallway, children's parlor, and library.

Carpet Installation: THE GFROERER RUG COMPANY, INC.

In the 19th century, installing wall-to-wall carpet required 27" long carpet strips of carpet to be sewn together by hand (meticulously matching often-intricate patterns) and then fitted to the dimensions of a room, taking into account irregularities such as the shape of the hearth and doorways. Everyone who installed carpet knew these skills. Today, there are only six people in America who still know how to hand-sew carpeting.

One of them is Robert Gfroerer, who, along with his son Bryan, owns and operates the Gfoerer Rug Company in Cincinnati, Ohio. The Art Association turned Gfroerer Rug to supervise the installation of carpet in Edwards Place during the restoration with the knowledge that it was hiring the absolute best in the business.

The Gfroerer Rug Company was founded in 1890 by Robert's great-grandfather, Joseph Gfroerer, and has remained in the same family for six generations. The company began by cleaning and repairing loose rugs and branched into residential carpet cleaning after World War II. In 1985, the company began doing historical restorations and installations. Widely acknowledged as the industry leader in historic carpet installation, Gfroerer has sewn and laid carpet for museums and historic sites throughout the United States, most notably in the Lincoln Bedroom of the White House.

The carpeting in Edwards Place was woven in Kidderminster, England, then shipped to Gfroerer, where it was hand-sewn. In January, 2015, a team from Gfroerer drove to Springfield and began the installation process. Padding was installed, then the carpeting was laid in each room, stretched tight, and tacked to the perimeter. The result is carpeting installed with the same skill and expertise employed when the Edwards family installed their carpets in 1857.

Drapery: EXCITING WINDOWS BY SUSAN DAY

Window dressing was an important part of middle-class décor in the 19th century. Drapery served the practical function of blocking drafts, enhancing privacy, and protecting the furniture from sunlight damage, but it also served as a cultural indicator of taste and means. Because textiles were expensive, the presence of several yards of costly fabric hanging from the windows was a tangible symbol of disposable income. And the stylish arrangement of that drapery signaled that someone in the house (usually the wife) was educated, discerning, and worldly enough to keep up with domestic fashions.

Although the restoration of Edwards Place in the 1940s included heavy red curtains at the windows, those curtains disappeared at some point over the decades, leaving the windows with a sadly bare appearance. An important part of the 21st century restoration process was to return drapery to the windows in order to accurately replicate the appearance of the house as the Edwards family experienced it.

The drapery in the sitting room were sewed by Bev Hafemeister of Vintage Valances in Cincinnati, Ohio. Shades of blue and green were selected to complement the color of the wallpaper and to pick up on highlights in the carpet. Because this room was generally used only by family, the drapery is less formal, with less ornate trimming.

Susan Day of Exciting Windows created the drapery for the rest of the first floor. Day has been creating stunning window treatments for almost 20 years and has won numerous national and international awards for her work. She is widely regarded as the best in the business and the Art Association was thrilled with her enthusiasm for the restoration process, understanding of the type of drapery being sought, and expertise in creating an historic look while staying within a budget.

Before restoration, Edwards Place lacked any drapery in its main rooms, giving it a bare appearance.

Day created an elegant blue curtain to hang in the space between the dining room and the adjacent archaeology exhibit. In the 19th century this space was likely a doorway, but at some point in the 20th century a large opening was created between the two rooms. This curtain between them can be opened to permit free flow between the rooms, but closed to maintain the illusion of the 19th century in the dining room. In the hallway, Day cleverly engineered drapery for the archway leading to the restroom, thus softening and improving an awkward space within the house.

The back hall and children's parlor received sheer curtains in a soft winter white. The simplicity of these curtains is in keeping with spaces within the house subject to a lot of wear and tear – the back hall from servants walking up and down the stairs, and the children's parlor from the Edwards' grandchildren playing with their toys.

Day's designs for the dining room (*left*) and hallway (*right*) and the finished products.

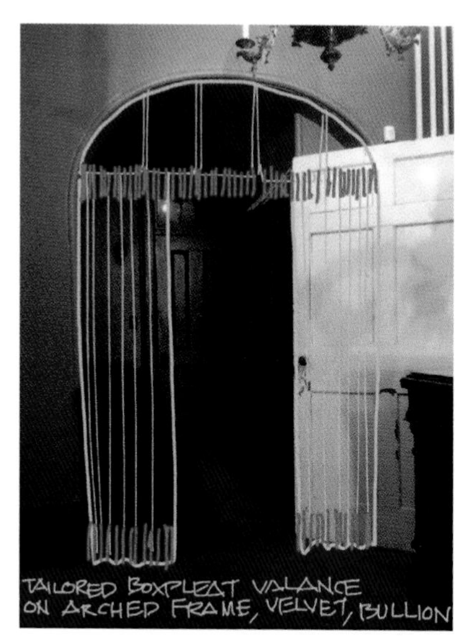

Sheers give the children's parlor an airy feel, while vertical blinds emphasize the library's masculine character.

Next page: Day's drapery creations for the formal parlors were inspired by 19th century designs.

As the most masculine room in the house, the library of Edwards Place received blinds stained a rich walnut and secured with a neutral twill tape. Venetian blinds were found in wealthier American households by the end of the 18th century. In the 19th century they became common in office settings to regulate light and air.

As the most formal rooms in the house, reserved almost exclusively for company, the two front parlors received the most expensive and elaborate window treatments in the house. With no surviving documentation as to what the Edwards family's drapery looked like, Day turned to *The Cabinet-Maker and Upholsterer's Guide* by George Smith, published in 1826, as a reference. Smith was the upholsterer to the British King George IV; the designs he created would have trickled down to middle-class American households by the second quarter of the nineteenth century.

Because both parlors would have functioned as a single space for entertaining, Day dressed both rooms in identical cobalt blue faux silk. In the music room, she adapted Smith's design for "drawing-room window curtains," employing a double-horned valance over side curtains and lace sheers. In the front parlor, she adapted a timeless design from the 1809 *The Upholsterer's Repository* that features an elaborately swagged and trimmed valance over side curtains and lace sheers, finished with ornate cornices from the Edwards Place collection.

Ultimately, Day created window treatments that are beautifully designed, expertly constructed, and flawlessly hung. They give Edwards Place the true feeling of stepping back into a time when no gentleman's house was considered complete without elegant drapery.

ROYAL BLUE SILK DAMASK – SEE
MRS. LINCOLN'S DRESSES. USE
SOLID FAUX SILK FOR COLOR/VOLUME

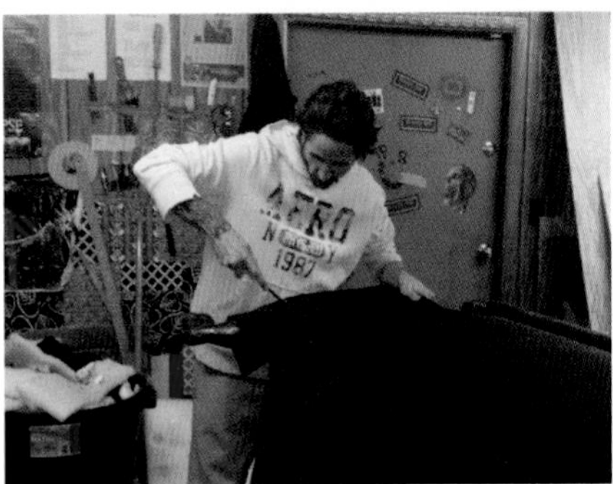

A c. 1820s sofa belonging to Governor Ninian Edwards was given a new lease on life after being reupholstered at Ash Street Upholstery.

Upholstery: ASH STREET UPHOLSTERY

The Edwards Place collection of decorative arts features an impressive array of 19th century antiques, many of which have Springfield connections or are original to the Edwards family. As part of the restoration process, several chairs and sofas with worn or historically inappropriate fabric were sent to Ash Street Upholstery. This full-service commercial and residential establishment, owned and operated by Barb and Bob O'Donnell, is one of the oldest and most respected upholstery shops in central Illinois. In business since 1960, Ash Street capably handles all aspects of upholstery, including sewing repairs, broken board repairs, cushion restuffs, or even rebuilding an antique from the frame up.

Three pieces of original Edwards family furniture (two chairs and a sofa) were reupholstered in black horsehair. Although the idea of fabric made from the manes and tales of horses is strange to modern minds, in the 19th century horsehair upholstery was prized for its sheen and durability and was extremely popular. The Edwards family bought furniture upholstered in black horsehair in the 19th century, as did the Lincoln family. Not only does black horsehair upholstery return these artifacts to their original appearance, it also allows visitors to Edwards Place to quickly identify which objects are original to the Edwards family.

Non-Edwards family antiques were reupholstered in dark blue, diamond-weave horsehair. Although there is no evidence that the Edwards family used this color or pattern, it is historically accurate, and moreover it serves the important function of distinguishing regular antiques from Edwards family belongings. Visitors to Edwards Place are invited to sit in these chairs for a more complete sensory experience of what life was like in the 19th century.

Appraisals and Auctioneer: GARTH'S AUCTIONS, INC.

One of the greatest strengths Edwards Place has as an historic site is its collection of artifacts, which includes significant early Illinois furniture, important 19th century portraits, the Thomas Condell ethnographic collection, as well as objects accumulated by the Art Association over the past century of its history.

The Edwards Place Committee of the Springfield Art Association spends significant time and energy curating its collection. In addition to making sure that objects are appraised, labeled, and documented, the Committee also periodically recommends adding objects to the collection through purchase or donation, and removing objects from the collection when they are redundant or do not serve the mission.

Andrew Richmond of Garth's Auctions did several appraisal events to benefit the restoration of Edwards Place.

Garth's Auctioneers and Appraisers in Columbus, Ohio has been a strong partner in helping the Art Association maintain the health of its permanent collections. Garth's has been a national force in the world of antiques and fine art since its founding by Garth Oberlander in 1954 and is now recognized as one of the top auction firms in North America. Garth's Vice President, Andrew Richmond, conducted an appraisal for insurances purposes over the course of several visits in 2013. While in town, Richmond was often kind enough to conduct public antiques appraisal events and donate the proceeds to the Edwards Place restoration fund, or to share his expertise on Midwestern antiques with the Springfield community through a public presentation.

The Edwards Place Committee also turned to Garth's to sell high-end objects deaccessioned from the permanent collection. Selling at auction allows each object to garner the maximum market value while removing any possibility of a conflict of interest in the object's disposal. With its Midwestern location, international audience, and commitment to customer service, Garth's

was able to offer low shipping costs, access to a broad customer base, and personal attention to detail that made the selling process smooth and profitable.

With its specialization in Midwestern antiques, Garth's auction house was the first place the Art Association looked when in the market to acquire new artifacts to bolster the interpretation of Edwards Place. The handsome Gothic bookcase in the library and four small wooden chairs in the children's parlor were all purchased at one of Garth's auctions.

A late 19th century desk was deaccessioned and sold by Garth's Auctions. Proceeds were used to purchase the Gothic-style bookcase, above, which is more period appropriate to the library of Edwards Place. *Photographs courtesy of Garth's Auctions.*

206

RENAISSANCE REVIVAL DESK.

American or European, late 19th-early 20th century, mahogany. Elaborately carved with figures, masks, and scrollwork. Older finish, some veneer damage. 32"h. 48.5"w. 27"d. Collected by Thomas Condell in Springfield, Illinois, in the early 20th century.
$1,000-$2,000

206

54 | GARTH'S January 26, 2013

Architect of Record:

WALTON AND ASSOCIATES ARCHITECTS, P.C.

For more than 30 years, the maintenance and historic character of Edwards Place have been in the capable hands of Don Walton, president and principal architect of Walton and Associates Architects, P.C.

As an associate with the firm of Ferry & Henderson, Walton oversaw the structural stabilization and restoration of Edwards Place in 1978-79. This extensive rehabilitation included repair to the millwork; tuckpointing of masonry; installing a new roof; reconstruction of the chimneys; reconstruction and repair of the front portico; repair of the shutters; restoration of the back porch to its 19th century appearance; and installation of an alarm system.

Walton was a natural choice to shepherd the interior restoration of Edwards Place as the architect of record. In addition to his work in the 1970s, Walton spent more than 10 years as the head of the Facilities and Grounds Committee, ensuring that Edwards Place remained stable and in good repair for future generations. As co-chairs of the Springfield Art Association's Centennial Capital Campaign Committee, Walton and his wife Carole have also been the driving force behind raising the requisite funds to make the restoration of Edwards Place possible.

Walton founded Walton and Associates in 1990 out of a desire to establish a deeper, personal interaction with his clients. WAA is an award-winning firm that offers a full range of professional services such as Long and Short Range Planning, Pre-Design, PCM, Programming, Interiors & Construction Delivery Services. Each of these services are custom tailored to meet the specific needs of each client, delivering a project that remains on schedule and within the budget while aligning with the vision and goals of the client.

Edwards Place

Chapter Seven

A Walk
THROUGH EDWARDS PLACE

THE EDWARDSES WERE FAMOUS FOR THEIR HOSPITALITY. Whether entertaining a few friends at a small dinner party or hundreds of visitors at a legislative reception, they delighted in bringing people together within the walls of their elegant home.

Now, with the house restored to its 1850s appearance, the Springfield Art Association is proud to continue the tradition of welcoming guests to Edwards Place. In an era where so much of our lives are lived in cyberspace – through our phones, our tablets, and our computers – a site like Edwards Place becomes ever more meaningful. It is a place where people take a breath, unplug, and literally step into history. It is a place where visitors can walk in the footsteps of people who lived a century and a half ago and see what they saw and touch what they touched. It is a place where the joys, sorrows, triumphs, and defeats of real people still echo through the centuries. It is a place to have the kind of visceral, moving experience that only happens when one comes into contact with a physical reminder of the past.

Edwards Place tells the story of life in 19th century Springfield. Within its walls, the world of hoop skirts and horse drawn carriages, of Benjamin Edwards and Abraham Lincoln, is alive and waiting to be experienced. Come join us on this journey...

An ornate hallstand such as this one would have given the Edwards family's guests a chance to check their appearance and hang up their coats and hats while visiting.

Stair Hall

To a middle-class family like the Edwardses, the front door was more than a front door: it was the divide that separated the haven of their home from the uncertainty of the outside world. The 19th century was a dynamic time. More and more people were giving up an agricultural way of life for an urban lifestyle that involved working outside the home. The population was booming, bringing people with unfamiliar habits and customs from all over the world. In the midst of these changes, the outside world was seen as cold, cruel, unprincipled, and callous, while the home was seen as a sanctuary; a safe haven, the center of everything that was good and moral and pure in life.

A visitor to Edwards Place would be greeted at the front door by one of the maids and ushered into the front hall to wait. The décor of the hall was carefully chosen with this waiting guest in mind; a grand staircase with a runner and stair rods, stylish wallpaper, luxurious carpet, elaborate wood trim with faux oak graining, and an ornate hallstand were all signals that the residents of this house were people of taste and means.

Stepping into the front hall is like stepping into the mind of a 19th century American. The layout of the house reflected the way that Victorian Americans conceptualized their home. To the left were the sitting room, dining room, and stairs leading to the bedrooms. These were "private," areas of the house, generally used only by family or close friends. To the right were the formal parlors, rooms set aside almost exclusively for company.

The back hall was the "service" area of the house, with a passageway leading to the kitchen and stairs leading up to the servants' quarters. The Edwards family drew a sharp visual distinction between the front and back halls to emphasize the difference in status between the family and servants. The trim in the back hall was painted a putty gray color rather than faux painted to resemble oak, and the back stairs were left uncarpeted.

The main hallway now affords modern visitors to Edwards Place a chance to peek at the original 1833 brick walls. A window into the plasterwork in the front hall opens to reveal gray-painted bricks that once formed the outside wall of the front of the house, while three windows in the back hall open to reveal whitewashed brick that once surrounded the back porch.

A window in the wall reveals the gray-painted brick that formed the exterior of the house prior to 157

As a utilitarian space reserved for the use of servants, the back hall was painted putty gray rather than faux-grained to resemble oak.

Next page: The formal entry hall was designed to impress visitors to Edwards Place with its scale and style.

Sitting Room

The sitting room was a place for the Edwards family to gather together and relax at the end of the day. The Victorian era saw a change in the way people viewed families. In colonial times, economic necessity bound families together as much as affection. In the 19th century, greater emphasis was placed on bonds of love within the family. Roles for men and women grew more distinct, too: men were seen as the providers who would go outside into the cold, cruel world and earn a living. Women were the guardians of all that was moral and pure and loving, who would work to make sure that the home was a soothing refuge from the outside world.

The Edwardses greatly valued the bonds of family. The sitting room was the emotional center of the home, where family relationships were cherished and nurtured. Here the family gathered in the evening to spend time together reading books and newspapers, writing letters, sewing, and playing games. Devout Presbyterians, they also used this room for family prayers after breakfast each morning. Today, portraits of Benjamin and Helen watch over the room where they had so many happy times as a family.

Because this room was seldom visited by outside guests, the wallpaper is quainter, and the furniture in this room is more mismatched and more comfortable, than the décor in the parlors. Benjamin's chair sat in the corner, and Helen's rocking chair sat by the fire. The large pier mirror is original to the home and still bears the label from its St. Louis manufacturer. The whatnot by the fireplace was donated by the Edwards grandchildren as a replica of one they remember in this room. A Bible belonging to Helen's brother Henry, who died in 1839 at age twenty-one, sits on the center table, inviting the family to gather around and study its passages together.

The Edwards family embraced Victorian values of family and religion. They spent countless nights together reading the family bible (above) around the center table in the sitting room.

Next page: The restored sitting room of Edwards Place.

Dining Room

The dining room was where the Edwards family took their meals, as well as where they entertained guests at elaborate dinner parties.

Dining underwent great changes in the years before the Civil War. The coming of the railroads and telegraph meant that exotic foods could be ordered and shipped from St. Louis or Chicago. The Edwardses' menus often included imported luxuries such as oysters and fresh fruit. Rules for dining also grew more elaborate. Whereas rural families often ate stews or other one-dish meals and often shared bowl and utensils; middle- and upper-class Victorian etiquette called for dinners with multiple courses and multiple dishes per course.

This gave rise to new utensils and dishes that were to be used with specific foods. "Genteel" people such as the Edwardses and their friends would

The buffet in the Edwards Place dining room dates to 1831. Atop it sits original Edwards family silver and glassware.

Previous page: A view of the dining room, looking into the sitting room.

have known all the rules of dining and felt comfortable in this setting; people who were not "well-bred" would not. The dining room is papered in a soft blue pattern that is more formal than the sitting room but less formal than the parlors. The small-pattern, ingrain carpeting represents a style that would have been easy to clean. Under the carpet is the remnant of a foot-operated call bell that Helen Edwards would have employed to summon her "dining room girl" between courses. The sideboard, built in 1831, once belonged to Springfield's founding family and is signed by the cabinetmaker, Thomas Estep. The silver- and glassware displayed on its surface is original to the family; many silver pieces bear the monograms of the Edwards' daughters. The dining room table started life as the Edwards family's Knabe square grand piano. In the early 20th century Alice Edwards salvaged the legs and had this table created.

Portraits of Norman, Lucy, and Lillie Judd painted by famed American artist George Peter Alexander Healy watch over the dining room. The large portrait of Lillie was painted after her untimely death at age 8 in 1865, leaving her grieving parents childless.

Alice Edwards Ferguson had the legs from her parents' old square grand piano made into the table that now sits in the dining room.

The remnants of a servants' call bell was found embedded in the floor of the dining room.

Next page: The restored dining room of Edwards Place.

Formal Parlors

For more than 60 years, the formal parlors were where the Edwards family entertained their visitors. Each winter, political luminaries would gather in this room at one of the Edwards' renowned legislative receptions. Abraham Lincoln, Stephen A. Douglas, Ulysses S. Grant, and several Governors of Illinois were among the honored guests. On quieter evenings, a select handful of friends might gather for a literary reading or to play parlor games. It was in this room that Benjamin Edwards displayed his famous hospitality and Helen showed off her skill as a hostess.

Music often enlivened these events. Helen Edwards, her mother, and her daughters all played the piano, but the musical talent seemed to have skipped the men in the family: Helen wrote that grandson Tom "is fond of music, and yet has no more idea of tune, than your Father." In the 19th century, being able to play the piano was often part of a well-bred young woman's education. A piano in the home was also an unmistakable sign of gentility, indicating that its owners had both the means buy this very expensive instrument as well as to the leisure to take lessons and play.

The upright grand piano in the first parlor was manufactured by Joseph Hisky of Baltimore and purchased by Springfield resident and United States Congressman William L. May around 1830. Its journey to Illinois from Baltimore - shipped by steamer from to New Orleans, then up the Mississippi River to St. Louis, then up the Illinois River to Beardstown, then overland 50 miles to Springfield – is indicative of the importance of music and culture to the lives of early western settlers. May sold this piano to Pascal P. Enos sometime in the mid1830s. It stayed in the Enos family until it was donated to the Art Association in 1952.

A rocking chair owned by Benjamin and Helen Edwards (*top*) and a square grand piano owned by Ninian and Elizabeth Edwards and topped by Helen's music book (*below*) grace the formal parlors.

The wallpaper in the parlor was reproduced from a c. 1850 fragment discovered during the course of restoration.

Next three pages: The parlors of Edwards Place, restored to the opulence of their heyday.

The square grand piano to the left of the fireplace was made by Emilius N. Scherr of Philadelphia. It originally belonged to Benjamin's brother and sister-in-law, Ninian and Elizabeth Edwards. Notes played on its ivory keys entertained a young Mary Todd when she was a houseguest in the Edwards home, as well as her beau, Abraham Lincoln. Family tradition holds that this piano played the music the night Abraham and Mary Lincoln were married. The sheet music atop this piano and in the nearby music stand date to the 1830s -1850s and belonged to Helen Edwards and her daughter, Helen Maria.

Portraits of Ninian and Elizabeth Edwards overlook another of their cherished possessions: the large, horsehair-upholstered sofa that once graced their parlors in the days when Lincoln visited to court Mary Todd. Recently restored to its 1840s appearance, the sofa now rests in Edwards Place as a tribute to the Lincolns. Visitors from across the street and across the world alike are drawn to this object, which represents one of the very few tangible remnants of an incredibly significant time in the Lincolns' lives.

In the second parlor, the black horsehair sofa and two chairs are original to the Edwards family. Tradition has it that they were purchased for use in this room when the Edwards family expanded their house in 1857. The large mirror reportedly came from the grand mansion of Ann Todd Smith, Mary Lincoln's sister, which was built in 1864 at the corner of Fourth and Cook Streets in Springfield.

As the room set aside for entertaining, the formal parlors were the very best room in the house, furnished the most expensively. Everything in these rooms, from the quality of the furnishings to the richness of the window treatments to the exuberance of the carpet and wallpaper - was carefully selected to make a good impression on company.

The library of Edwards Place contains many books original to the family, all of whom were well-educated and enjoyed reading.

Library

Home libraries were a luxury for only an elite few in the 19th century. Most houses simply weren't spacious enough to devote an entire room to books, and most budgets weren't large enough to purchase the number of books that would necessitate an entire room to store them. The presence of a library in Edwards Place reflects the Edwards family's wealth as well as the value they placed on literacy.

Every member of the Edwards family was well-educated. Benjamin had attended college and law school at Yale, and was the first person born in Illinois to graduate from that institution. Helen attended local schools in New York and New Haven as a child and received French lessons from a private tutor. Daughter Helen was sent to the Monticello Female Seminary in Godfrey, Illinois, and her sisters Alice and Mollie attended Springfield schools for ladies. The family loved to read and frequently discussed their books with each other. Their letters also make frequent mention of evenings spent reading aloud. In 1856, for example, Benjamin wrote his daughter Helen that "I bought *Dr Kanes Arctic Expedition* and commenced reading it aloud last night to Mother. We think it very interesting." In 1868, Alice's letter to her sister mentioned that her husband "...is reading out loud 'Vanity Fair,' I think it is one of the finest novels I have ever heard read."

The library also likely served as a home office for Benjamin to work on legal documents for his court cases. Benjamin was a prominent attorney for more than 40 years. He and John T. Stuart started doing business together under the name of Stuart & Edwards in 1843; the firm became Stuart, Edwards, and Brown when Christopher C. Brown joined the firm in 1860. This firm is still in business. Now called Brown, Hay, and Stephens, it is recognized as the oldest law firm in Illinois. In addition to his work as a lawyer, Benjamin served one term as judge of the Sangamon County Circuit Court from 1869-70 and served as president of the Illinois State Bar Association from 1885—1886.

According to the Edwards' granddaughter Eliza, the library was a private space in the house. Unless the family was hosting a very large reception, the pocket doors were kept closed with a sofa in front of them, and the room was accessed from the side hall. Bookcases lined the wall and a table with a gas lamp sat in the center of the room. Today the library is carpeted with a bold Gothic pattern to emphasize the masculine and academic nature of this room. Two original Gothic chairs upholstered in black horsehair are complemented by a desk and bookcase with arched windows. A large Gothic bookcase, also original to the house, is filled with the Edwards family's books. The elegant black sofa, recently reupholstered in black horsehair, belonged to Governor Ninian Edwards in the 1820s and is one of the oldest antiques in the house. Forming the backdrop for it all is a reproduction of the original wallpaper pattern first hung in this room in 1857. A fragment of this paper survives and has been preserved for comparison on the southeast wall.

Above: An original Edwards family chair sits in front of surviving and reproduced 1850s wallpaper.

Below, left: Benjamin Edwards likely did legal work at a desk such as this one in the library.

Below, right: Governor Ninian Edwards's Classical Revival sofa sits in the library, just as it did during the Edwards family's occupancy.

Next two pages: Views of the library of Edwards Place.

Top: archaeological fragments of child-sized teacups and plates that belonged to Helen Maria Edwards in the 1840s. *Bottom*: Period examples of Halma and Martelle, two games enjoyed by the Edwards family.

Children's Parlor

"The fourth room, way at the back, was the children's playroom where all our toys and things were kept," recalled Eliza Condell of the northernmost room on the first floor of Edwards Place. The Edwardses' first grandchild was born in 1863, and they continued arriving at regular intervals until the last one was born in 1885. In all, there were ten surviving grandchildren: Tom, Eddie, Helen, Eliza, Alice, and Mary Condell (Helen's children); and Ned, Bess, Helen, and Miner Raymond (Mollie's children). All ten children were frequent guests at Edwards Place. The Raymonds would visit from Evanston in the summer with their mother, and the Condells would live with their grandparents during the academic year so they could attend Springfield schools.

In colonial times, children were seen, at worst, as sinful and corrupt beings, at best, as defective, miniature adults. The playroom reflects the sentimental view of children and childhood embraced by Victorian Americans in the 19th century. Inspired by the likes of Charles Dickens, Charlotte Bronte, and Queen Victoria, children were now seen as spiritually pure creatures, as yet uncorrupted by the world, and childhood was considered a happy, innocent time that must be celebrated and prolonged. Victorian culture placed great emphasis on the role of motherhood for women, at the same time industrialization brought middle-class mothers more disposable income and a greater array of toys available for purchase. The period witnessed a significant increase in the volume of paintings, books, toys, advice manuals, and other things designed specifically with children in mind.

Evidence tells us that the Edwards' children and grandchildren had a wide variety of things to play with. In a delightful letter to a granddaughter written in 1901, Helen described "...a large walnut box in the north room... filled full & heavy with other games & cards of many years gathering. Game of

Authors, The Bushy Cards, Togemorhy, Old Maid, Peter Coddle's Visit to New York – heaps & heaps of them." Other letters mention grandchildren playing with parlor croquet, alphabet blocks, and a rocking horse. The children's playroom is furnished with antique examples of as many of these toys and games as could be located. They are all available for visitors to handle.

The wallpaper in this room is a reproduction of the pattern originally hung in 1857, when this room ceased being a kitchen and was turned into formal living space. Small fragments of original wallpaper, as well as shadows of the pattern imprinted on the plaster, tell us that this room was papered in the same pattern as the adjacent library.

Above: A china doll once owned by one of the Edwards daughters. *Left:* Antique examples of the toys and pastimes once owned by the Edwards family are available for visitors to examine.

Next two pages: The children's parlor of Edwards Place is now a bright, inviting space for children to play games of the past.

Thank You

TO THE GENEROUS SUPPORTERS OF EDWARDS PLACE

The Springfield Art Association has been overwhelmed at the generosity of its friends, members, and neighbors, who have donated their time and resources to the cause of restoring Edwards Place to the grandeur of its heyday. The result is an historic site that is not just a memorial to the people and events of the past, but a living monument to the spirit of generosity and community that made its restoration possible.

Special thanks must be extended to Mr. Tom Jeffris and the JEFFRIS FAMILY FOUNDATION. Headquartered in Janesville, Wisconsin, its mission is to preserve the cultural history and heritage of the Midwest through the preservation of regionally and nationally important historic buildings and decorative arts projects. Without the Foundation's generous award of a planning grant and two challenge grants, this restoration would not have been possible.

Thanks also to PATRICIA AND DON ALTORFER, whose generous contribution allowed us to reach our fundraising goal two years ahead of schedule. We are deeply grateful to your continued support of and belief in Edwards Place and the Springfield Art Association.

The Art Association is also grateful to the THE SHELBY CULLOM DAVIS CHARITABLE FUND for its support of this project. Benjamin S. Edwards was the law mentor of Shelby Cullom Davis's distinguished ancestor, Illinois Governor Shelby Cullom.

Finally, the Art Association would like to thank THE COMMUNITY FUND OF THE LAND OF LINCOLN for the award of an historic preservation grant to support the reproduction of historic wallpaper.

THANKS ALSO TO:

Dawn and Jim Abraham
Leslie and Angie Acakpo-Satchivi
Sarah and Bryan Albracht
Ingrid Alexander
Shawn Andrews and Clay Crocker
Anonymous Donors
Judy and Jim Antonacci
Dr. Jane and Steven Arbuthnot
Kathy and Michael Badger
Kate and Joe Baima
Bonnie A. Barber
Judith Barringer and Rich Kerhlikar
In Memory of Winifred Barringer
Jennifer Baur
In Memory of Jim Baur
Sandy Bellatti
Marjorie Berchtold
Mary Lynn Perkins and Jim Bertram
Jennifer and Chad Bettis
Elaine Birtch
In Memory of Dr. Alan Birtch
Mark Birtch and Kim Elliott-Birtch
Beverly Brekke-Bailey
Pam and James Brown
Hillary Bunn
Sarah and Bob Brown
Mary Beth and Bob Burke
Larry A. Bussard
Frank Butterfield
Ryan Cadagin
Gael Carnes
Joan and Don Casper
In Memory of Aletha Staab
Octavia and Peter Casper, Sr.
Kristin and Peter Cavanagh
Julie and Bill Cellini
Denise Church
Lindsey Arbuthnot Clancey
Community Foundation for the Land of Lincoln
Anna and Timothy Daly
Carolyn Davis
Shelby Cullom Davis Charitable Fund
Megan Davis Flanary
Bonnie and Douglas Dee
Paula and Thomas Denny
Barbara Dickerman
Lori and David Dodwell
Betsy Dollar
Jana Van Fossan Dreyzehner and John Dreyzehner
In Memory of Vickie Van Fossan
Carolyn and Dan Dungan
Myto Duong
R.W. Troxell & Company
Tad Edwards
Joyce and Jim Edwards
In Memory of Julia Edwards
Diane and Jim Edwards
Jennifer and Jeff Egizii
Shelly and Chris Ehrlich
Susan and Bill Enlow
Enos Park Neighborhood Association
Bronwyn and Bill Eves
Phyllis and George Fairchild
Daniel Farmer
Fletcher Farrar and Mary Jessup
Dave, Ruth, and Nora Fickes
Hazen and Roland Folse
Carla Kloppenburg Foreman
Eleanor and Fred Frank
Roy French
Kelsi Frost
Ann and Farrell Gay
Katherine and Randy Germeraad
Jeff and Susan Gibbs
Ed Gonet, Gonet Designs Corporation
Patricia and Donald Graham
Taryn and Sean Grant
Amy and Shane Harris
Barbara Hartman
Lynn and Harris Hatcher
In Memory of Clarice Hickox
Barbara and John Hayes
Margaret Suggs Herath
Nancy Roberts Herndon
In Memory of Florence Grigsby Roberts
Mary Lou Hicks and Cathy Yeaman
Joseph Hills
Erika Holst and Christopher Schnell
In Memory of Jim and Ingeborg Rozinek
Betty and Ralph Hurwitz
Illinois Prairie Pastel Society
Jane and Steve Jackman
Renee and Bradley Johnsen
In Honor of Barbara Brunk Harris
Kerianne and Kyle Johnson
In Honor of Judy Johnson
Cindy Jordan
Julie and Scott Kaiser
Sandra Yeh and Gregory Kane
Jackie and Mike Kelly
Marilyn Schnirring Kennedy
Kirsten and Joe Kienzler
Cinda Schien-Kincade, Courtney, and Christopher Kincade
In Honor of June and Lou Myers
Lynn and George King
Dana and Steve Kinion
Margaret Kirschner
Chris Klaus
Ban Kloppenburg
Margot Kramer

Ann Kramer
Julie and Tom Krehbiel
In Memory of Bruce Ratterree
Cyd and Rob LaBonte
Allison Lacher and Nathan Steele
Bill Lazarus
Rosemary and Bob Leistner
Meaghan Lloyd
Jane, Lucy, and Phil Locascio
Marissa Gibbs Lorance
Elly and Boyd Mackus
Tracey Maras
In Memory of Betsy Carlson
Sally and Russ Martin
Marilyn M. Maurer
Lisa and Chris McDowell
Diane McEvoy
Debbie and Ted Megginson
Kelly and Matt Minder
Janet and Leon Mizeur
Linda and Kriegh Moulton
Elizabeth and Sergio Murer
Mrs. Phillip G. Murray
Gavin Myers
The Louis Shaver Myers Family
Teena and Michael Myers
Terri and Steve Myers
Katherine C. Narmont
Christine Niemann
Gail Noll and John Milhiser
Theresa O'Hare
Lynne and Paul O'Shea
Carl Ostermeier
Rebecca and Richard Owens
Carolyn Oxtoby
Margie Paoletti
Sherry and Jim Park
J'Amy and Bill Payne
Mary and Harold Perkins
In Memory of Dr. and Mrs. Emmet Pearson and Thomas Pearson
Carole and Phillip Peterson
Marci and Nick Petropoulos
Melinda Bunn Pfeffer
Alice Prickett
Sheri and Don Ramsey
Miner Raymond
Sarah Elizabeth Reid
Bitsy and Bill Reisch
Priscilla Reyhan
Rose Marie Roach
Sula and Mark Roberts, Jr.
Elizabeth and Henry Rohs
Alice and David Rolf
Jourdan Rothschild
David Reid and Dr. Beth Strow
Anthony Rubano
Peggy and Tom Ryder
Sue and Steve Scaife
Maureen and Robert Schaaf
Craig Schermerhorn
Lori and Bill Schlosser
Martha C. Schneerman
Lisa Schnell
In Memory of Margit Rogers
Kathy and Milton Sees
Carole and James Shay
Larry Shiner and Catherine Walters
Marsha Shomidie
Jennifer Simons
Dianne O'Keefe Simpson
Elizabeth Small and Stanley Herrin
Mary-Leigh Call Smart
In Memory of Mary B.
CallMichael John Smith
Donna J. Solomon
Polly Spengler
Spoon River Group
Springfield Electric Supply Company
Fund of the Community Foundation for the Land of Lincoln
Mary and David Stjern
Lisa and Stephen Stone
E. Cori Stuart
Guerry Suggs and Jo Alessandrini
Nicky Stratton
Neta and Stephen Tagge
John Terril, Terril & Company
Susan Ostermeier Tesar
Evelyn Brandt Thomas
Rachael and Mike Thomson
Susan Thrasher
In Memory of Drs. Ann and Raymond Pearson
Springfield Tracy Fund of the Community Foundation for the Land of Lincoln
Mary and Bob Trask
Eloise and Don Van Fossan
Barbara Walker
Carole and Don Walton
Kate and Justin Ward
Karen and Bob Westbrook
Diana Widicus and Michael Davis
Martha Clements Wilday
In Memory of Doris Kruse Clements
Linda and Brett Wolters

Source Material

MANUSCRIPT COLLECTIONS

Anna Ridgely Hudson Diary, Abraham Lincoln Presidential Library (ALPL)
Condell Family Papers, ALPL
Conkling Family Papers, ALPL
Dresser Family Papers, ALPL
Eliza Condell Interviews, n.d., Springfield Art Association (SAA)
Elizabeth Capps Papers, SAA
Land Tract Sales Database, Illinois State Archives
Record Group 21, Records of the District Courts of the United States, National Archives
Orville H. Browning diary
Queenie Ryan Papers, SAA
Stuart-Hay Papers, ALPL

NEWSPAPERS

Illinois State Journal
Illinois State Register
New York Times
Sangamo Journal

ARTICLES AND BOOKS

Angle, Paul. *Here I Have Lived: A History of Lincoln's Springfield.* Springfield, Illinois: The Abraham Lincoln Association, 1935.

Brown, Caroline Owsley. "Springfield Society Before the Civil War." *Journal of the Illinois State Historical Society* Volume 15, Nos. 1-2 (1922): 477-500.

Catron, Virginia Sinclair, and Mary Masters. "Edwards Place in Lincoln's Springfield." *The Magazine Antiques,* July, 1945.

Edwards, Georgie Hortense. *Historical Sketches of the Edwards and Todd Families*. Springfield, Illinois: H.W. Rokker, 1895.

"Mrs. Helen K. Dodge Edwards." *Journal of the Illinois State Historical Society* Volume 2, Number 1, (1909): 34-37.

Pease, Theodore Calvin, and James Randall, eds. *The Diary of Orville Hickman Browning, Volume 1: 1850-1864.* Springfield, Illinois: Illinois State Historical Library, 1925.

Raymond, Mary Edwards, ed. "Some Incidents in the Life of Mrs. Benjamin S. Edwards." Privately published, 1909.

Smith, Dwight. "The Attempted Potawatomi Emigration of 1839." *Indiana Magazine of History* Volume 45, Issue 1, pp. 51-80.

Wilson, Douglas L., ed.; Davis, Rodney O., ed.; Edwards, Elizabeth; Edwards, Ninian W. "Elizabeth and Ninian W. Edwards (Jesse W. Weik Interview*)" in 'Herndon's Informants: Letters, Interviews, and Statements About Abraham Lincoln.'* Urbana: University of Illinois Press, 1998.

Woodward, Elizabeth Raymond. "Portrait of my Grandmother, Mrs. Lincoln's Kinswoman." *Journal of the Illinois State Historical Society* Volume 4, Number 1 (1948): 265-80.

Acknowledgements

The restoration of Edwards Place has been a labor of love undertaken by many talented and dedicated individuals, and documenting the story of that restoration in this book has been a sheer joy.

Special thanks are due to Betsy Dollar, Executive Director of the Springfield Art Association, for her wise counsel, unfailing support, artistic eye, hard work, and most of all for her visionary leadership, which has inspired a renaissance at the Art Association.

Thanks also to the staff of the Art Association. Jan Arnold, Mary Beth Burke, Charlotte Kane, and Erin Svendsen advised on content, proofread copy, supplied me with information, and just generally were supportive of an occasionally moody curator during the restoration of the house and the creation of this book.

The Springfield Art Association's Board of Directors has been unfailingly encouraging and enthusiastic about all facets of the restoration of Edwards Place. Thank you to its members, past and present.

The Centennial Capital Campaign Committee has worked tirelessly to raise the funds that made this restoration possible. Thank you to Sarah Albracht, Ingrid Alexander, Steve Arbuthnot, Judith Barringer, Tricia Becker, Mary Beth Burke, Betsy Dollar, Bronwyn Eves, Ellen Fliss, Jeff Gibbs, Dana Kinion, Jane Locascio, Steve Myers, Rich Owens, David Reid, and Don and Carole Walton.

I am deeply grateful to the Edwards Place Committee: Heather Barnhart, Judith Barringer, Frank Butterfield, Clay Crocker, Bronwyn Eves, Angela Goebel-Bain, Laura Reyman and Anthony Rubano. Edwards Place is as stunning as it is now because of the wisdom, commitment, and enthusiasm that these remarkable individuals displayed on a consistent basis throughout the course of the restoration process.

As Chair of the Edwards Place Committee, Anthony Rubano deserves singular credit. His exacting standards, attention to detail, historical expertise, and dedication to this project ensured that the results of this restoration are nothing short of spectacular. We are extremely lucky to have his guidance.

Clay Crocker also deserves special thanks. Clay is a woodworking genius who rose to the occasion several times over to deliver brilliantly designed and skillfully executed carpentry work to enhance the interpretation of the house. The windows into the walls in the main hall and the shelves, false door, and mantel in the archaeology room are all examples of Clay's handiwork.

Amanda Gleason is to be commended for laying the groundwork that culminated in the restoration of Edwards Place.

The restoration of Edwards Place was undertaken by a collection of incredibly talented individuals. Jay Brault, Mark Conaway, Bret Dalby, Susan Day, Alex DeMaris, Rick DeSollar, Ben Dodson, Don Evans, Wen Fritsch, John Gabriel, Bryan Gfroerer, Denny Gillette, Ed Gonet, Jeff Hawk, Tom Jennings, Mark Jones, Mike Jones, Kenny Lamotte, Brad Lynn, Jake Mahon, Trent Metzger, Wade Metzger, Ed Midden, Barb O'Donnell, Jason Olar, Charles Pell, Steve Sagle, Travis Savage, Robert Smith, Abby Styber, Don Walton and Gerry Whalen are all the best at what they do, and it has been my privilege to watch them apply their skills. Thank you for bringing this house back to life.

Thank you to Anna Lowethal for the gorgeous photos she took for this book.

And finally, my thanks and my heart belong to the Schnell boys, who are my everything.

Erika Holst